D0105827

Open Your Mind And Say "AHA"

Medicine for the 21st Century

By
Leonard Torok

ISBN 0-9772266-0-3

LCCN 2005931425

Printed in the United States of America

Contents

Foreword

One consistent finding in the history of medicine over the last several centuries has been animosity between the competing schools of allopathic (western) and homeopathic medicine. The disdain between these two groups of physicians has ruled out cooperation. Due to this lack of cooperation, the understanding of all physicians about how to choose the ideal treatment for their patients and their understanding of the treatment's mechanism of action has suffered right along with their patients.

Hopefully, the modern age of technology and high speed global communication can end this lack of cooperation. This book is an attempt to bridge the gap. My experience practicing medicine indicates that both the medical practitioner and his patient can benefit greatly from having all the options considered and available when a symptom or disease presents itself for treatment.

The medical practitioners of the future need to have available for their use an integration of the seemingly opposite thought processes inherent in taking either a physical or an energetic approach to understanding health. Every human being fully integrates both of these capabilities for their benefit. The medical sciences need to become equally holistic in their understanding of the mechanisms of health and disease.

This transformation of the medical profession must start with education and a willingness to be open-minded in your search for the truths of healing. Gaining experience with this integrated approach has proved to my great satisfaction that whatever efforts you might expend in this direction will repay you greatly with time.

After the principles of healing have been presented, a practical example of applying these principles to common health problems will be explored. This example will be the presentation of a holistic approach to understanding and treating common physical symptoms whose cause is fear. As more experience is gained with holistic healing in the future, further examples of how you can heal yourself of other common diseases will be presented (like obesity, diabetes or heart disease).

Introduction

You can heal. You can heal yourself. You can stay healthy. This is true. Now, *how* can you do all these things? My intention in writing this book is to enable you to discover the healing process that is naturally available to you and to understand the reasons why you have your current state of health.

Learning and applying nature's principles of healing should be an exciting process of self-discovery that allows you to learn why events come into your life and why they cause you either health or disease. The endpoint of your exploration is to recognize a path that represents the natural world's journey towards improving your health.

In this book you will be challenged to evaluate your life experiences from the optimistic viewpoint that every experience contains potential for your growth. The potential for growth and healing contained in every event of your life may be primarily physical, mental or emotional, but it will always be holistic. Each of these components of the holistic you can simultaneously achieve some measure of growth in the healing process and purpose of your life.

The various chapters of this book will focus on the steps you can learn that relate to your healing and health. The theories of western systems of medicine will be used as the starting point for evaluating other systems of medicine. These views will be assumed to already be familiar to the reader.

The theoretical principles contained within alternative systems of medicine will be investigated when they offer you a more complete understanding of the *underlying reason* of why a disease state is present. Your highest goal then becomes to be able to select a form of treatment that has the greatest potential for being curative because it deals with the cause of the disease.

To reach this goal, you will need to become familiar with the various treatment options you have and the reasons to choose one over another. After reviewing the principles and results achieved by alternative treatment approaches, you can make an assessment about the desirability of each approach. In the process of making treatment choices, objectivity is desirable but the author's current level of experience and biases, as well as your own, will naturally play a role in determining the final choice.

You will want to judge the new concepts you are being presented with against your own experiences and the biases these experiences have created in you. The challenge and opportunity being presented you is to stimulate your growth in understanding the healing process.

Several of the later chapters will end with some speculative imaginings. These are intended only for the purpose of stimulating your own speculative thinking. Each reader will have to blend the information with his or her own experiences in life and unique personality. This is because even though much is already known, some unanswered questions will still remain.

Better answers to the questions intended for your exploration in this book about healing can be achieved by adding your viewpoint to the total sum of knowledge and experiences currently available.

Keep these questions in your mind as you read on:

What is the true cause of your present symptoms and your state of health?

Why and how does healing occur or not occur?

What types of treatment have the highest potential to recover your optimal health because they can deal with the underlying cause of your symptoms?

Open Your Mind And Say "AHA"

Medicine for the 21st Century

Your Healing Heart

AWARENESS

All Healing is Self-Healing

Law of Similars =
The Healing Law of Nature

Healing = Transforming
Susceptibility into Resistance

Vital Force = "The Big You"

The Disease of Fear

ACCEPTANCE

Changing Your Perception of Reality

Being Open-Minded to
Alternative Views of Reality

It's OK to Talk to Yourself
and Listen to Your Body

The Amazing Human Being

Western Medicine has Value
as a Healing System

FORGIVENESS

The Meaning of Symptoms and Disease

You're OK

Healing: The Never Ending Story
= Learning and Healing Through
Life's Opportunities and Challenges

Chapter 1

Healing May Require a Change in Your Perception of Reality

If you've ever wondered why you have the health problems you do, this book is for you. If you wonder why other people have the health problems they do, this book is for you. If you ever suspected there must be a simpler or more powerful way to recover your health, this book is for you.

As you ask yourself these questions, you will be help greatly in formulating your answer to admit that you probably have only one way of looking for the answers. Based on more than three decades of the study and practice orthopedic surgery, Chinese medicine and homeopathic medicine, you will be presented alternative ways to find answers to these important questions.

Each of these three medical sciences has its own method of understanding the reasons why you have the health you do. They also each make use of different types of treatment to recover good health. This fact introduces a few new questions. How is it that three entirely different approaches to understanding health can all work in their own distinct way to heal the same diseases? If there is more than one way to heal, what is the best way to heal and what makes it the best?

In this book you will be challenged to learn the best way to heal yourself, just the same as my patients have challenged me to heal them in the best way. You will need to learn some new rules about the healing process. It will be helpful for you to be open-minded and accept the possibility that your current understanding of why you are sick may not be accurate or at least not the whole truth.

If you or someone dear to you, has a health condition that has been present for longer than six weeks, you have failed in healing. You would be well advised to open up your mind to an alternative approach or an alternative understanding of the reason for your failure to heal. You must accept the reality that you have failed to heal with the tools and knowledge that you have chosen so far. There are other treatment choices available and the purpose of this book is to help you understand how they work and when to choose them.

Involving yourself in a comparative study of the relative benefits of western, Chinese and homeopathic medicine will demand two things: first, you need to make an honest appraisal of the merits of your current understanding of the healing process. Familiarity will naturally tend to give you a favorable prejudice towards what you already understand. Second, you should strive to keep an open mind to the question: **Is it possible to change your perception of reality and is this necessary to improve your health and enjoyment of life?**

Your answer to this question should be yes if you have failed to fully maintain or recover good health. Even if your health is perfect, the information gained from studying the healing process can help you prevent future problems. Investing in yourself and your health is one of the more productive investments you can make.

Though it may at first glance appear that this book is a story about my life, it is really all about you and your life. Keep this in mind as you read and it will set the stage for your self-transformation into better health. If that seems like a tall order, because your health is not really very good at this time, don't worry, it is all quite achievable.

To reach this goal of improving your health, you need to learn some new rules about what factors shape your state of health. With this new information in hand, I would encourage you to be persistent in your application of these new principles.

Symptoms and stress are a part of life. The ultimate goal of this study is to learn how to turn symptoms and stress into tools to improve your health. Applying the new principles you will learn can help you select the best treatments to recover your health from among all the available treatment choices. It is important to carefully observe how you feel when applying these new principles. What at first might seem simple can become quite profound. It is necessary that you make an honest assessment of your current ideas and keep an open mind in evaluating the results of your new experiences.

The health benefits contained in these principles are within the capability of all people. *Do not think that you are greater or less than anyone else in your ability to recover optimal health!* We all have different starting points on the road to recovery, but we all share these same methods of making progress as well as the same desired goal. My experiences treating patients have shown me that it is indeed realistic for everyone to have optimism about their chances for recovery.

There are two important areas in which you should direct your attention. First will be to study the *principles* that determine why you have your present state of health. Second is to learn proven *processes* that allow you to take advantage of the principles you just learned about how to improve your health. The later chapters in the book will give you the tools you need to learn and apply these principles. You will start with learning how to "see" a new vision of the reasons why you have the current symptoms you do.

Remember the first question—"Is it possible to change your perception of reality and is this necessary to improve your health and enjoyment of life?" The answer is yes for the vast majority of American patients and physicians. This is particularly true if you are experiencing a chronic disease (symptoms present for more than six weeks).

Lets start by examining how your **perception** of the events occurring in your life can work to shape your state of health. The emphasis will be more on your **process** of perceiving the events than the events themselves. When you are able to perceive the underlying cause of your symptoms, you have the potential to treat at a more powerful level. When you treat the cause of your symptoms and not just the secondary symptoms, you can expect the results to produce more positive changes in your health. Your recovery can be more holistic and will be more permanent.

The goal is to enhance your ability to have more than one way of perceiving the events in your life. Improved health will follow from your being able to see equal value in different, and even opposite, interpretations of the events occurring in your life. Be open-minded. Try to suspend whatever rigidity you have in thinking that the cause of your health could have only one interpretation.

It is important to recognize that once you view the same event from an entirely different perspective, that same event will have a very different appearance. Both view of the same event are accurate but they are not the same. Having the freedom to make choices based on more than one view of reality will empower you to regain control over your health.

It will be helpful in starting this process of seeing different perspective to examine how you "see". What you see determines what your truth is. Having the ability to see more than one perspective of "reality" will enable you to practice seeing different truths and developing alternative ways of responding to life's challenges. A good place to start will be with a discussion of what is reality, or better yet, what is your present perception of reality.

"Get real". This is a common expression of today's generation. This phrase offers a nice perspective on your getting past denial that other perspectives of reality exist and that you have a natural tendency to create false illusions. Your past experiences, your personality and your prejudices will result in you seeing a different reality than others see. "Getting real" will be your starting point to re-examine your entire perception of reality. How you perceive the events of your life will determine what choices are available to you in recovering and maintaining good health.

It is important to take advantage of the knowledge that you will usually have your own individual way of seeing things. You have acquired this perspective based upon your unique personality and the individual experiences in life that have shaped you. This is easy to see repeated daily in life. For example, when you go shopping with someone else you hardly ever pick the exact same brand, style or color of a clothing item. You each have your own criteria for what looks the best to you. The choices you make will be unique but there will be some common principles underlying those choices.

If the goal is achieving better health, it will be helpful to examine why you make the treatment choices you do. You do have options, and should look at the process of how you choose a treatment option and each option's short and long term consequences. As you learn about and practice seeing different perspectives, you will have more opportunities for a successful recovery.

A physician is presented with a similar circumstance when he learns that there is more than one equally valid interpretation of the cause or meaning of a patient's symptoms or when a new treatment is introduced that offers equal or better results. Medical research frequently introduces new treatment options that require decisions be made based on the advantages and disadvantages of the old and new treatments. Learning new theories and new treatments can lead to having new experiences in seeing patients heal. When these new and different treatments for the same symptoms achieve equally satisfactory results, this creates a "dilemma" of choice.

Once you recognize that you have choices for your treatment, it demands that you critically evaluate the results of various treatments. As you gain experience with the results of more than one treatment option, your understanding of why particular results follow each type of treatment will be enhanced. This helps you approach a deeper level of understanding of the cause of symptoms. The closer a treatment is directed at the cause of a disease, the more likely it becomes that an "ideal" treatment option can be selected.

This book is intended to provide you with the information necessary to learn the benefits and risks of the various treatment options you have. Whatever effort you expend in learning the basis for making your treatment selections will pay off in better health, less suffering and less expense. You become an active and informed participant in your health care decisions. This becomes an empowerment that will always stay with you.

My impression is that in the last twenty years the patient has moved farther away from true "informed consent" due to the expanding complexity of medicine. The intrusion of government and insurance companies into the treatment decision process has further removed patients and their doctors from decisions that relate to what treatment is offered. Treatments are often mandated by a "standard of care" that leaves no options for individualization. All patients with a certain diagnosis are understood to have the same cause of their condition. It is hard to deviate from this "standard of care" without a lot of extra paperwork to document why a different choice of treatment was selected. Insurance companies may have contracts with health care providers that make it difficult for the physicians to offer more than one option for any problem. This situation of limiting your treatment options has been developed as an effort to control costs using the smokescreen of standardizing care.

In classical medicine, the role of the physician was as both a teacher and practitioner. When a patient receives the information necessary to understand his choices, both patient and physician equally benefit. The patient recovers and will be strengthened in a way that he chooses for himself. He will not be as totally dependent upon the medical system. The doctor will benefit in having his method of choosing treatments validated in the patient's results. He can see his patients recover with various treatments and judge the quality of the recovery. This will bring both the patient and physician closer to an understanding of the "reality" of healing. It brings the patient better health and the physician greater success and fulfillment in his practice. The only added cost is the time necessary to learn.

So, *what is the reality or truth of healing as it relates to what is* **causing** your symptoms or state of health? Hopefully, you will find this a fascinating question. One can take different approaches to answering that question. The concrete answer comes from a literal interpretation of the information you receive from your five senses, filtered through our mind. The intuitive answer adds different possibilities and hidden meanings beyond the information received from your five senses.

To help understand the different approaches to healing, I will present examples of how my view of reality changed as I gained knowledge and experience in alternative medicine. One fact or idea is not enough to change your view of reality. Each chapter of the book presents a step in the process of learning how to expand your view. At the end of the book, you should be a little farther along the path towards understanding the meaning of your state of health. As you learn how to learn, by focusing on the healing process, all subsequent lessons should be easier.

Reality just is what it is, regardless of the current perspective you are using to understand it. I learned one reality initially in medical school. Studying Chinese medicine presented a very different view of the reality of health. Homeopathic medicine again presents a completely different understanding of the meaning of symptoms and disease. As my perception and understanding of reality changed through education and experience, it did not represent any change in what is reality at all. Reality just is.

As I learned different options to relieve my patient's symptoms, it became necessary to reconcile the differences between opposing views of the reasons for their diseases and their healing. Reading this book will present you with this same challenge. I encourage you to read on with an open mind and a brave heart. Additional knowledge can offer an exciting opportunity to improve one's life, but it also presents some uncertainty.

When the basis you are using to make decisions becomes superseded by a different paradigm, it takes firm resolve to apply the new rules. It is common to hold on to a familiar understanding, just because it is familiar, even when you realize that its underlying premise may be wrong. This is even true when the results will directly impact your health. This becomes exaggerated when another person has placed their trust in you to do the best for them that you are able.

My training and career has been primarily in orthopedic surgery. This is a profession where one would not be well served to be lacking in confidence or have self doubt about how you are to do your job. Surgeons daily take people apart with the full anticipation that they will put them back together better than when they started. Due to the serious implications of any treatment plan that is chosen, the pace at which I changed my life may be a little slower than what you are able to achieve. It may be more important to be sure you are going in the right direction than how quickly you might be scurrying along your path.

I have been fortunate in my career to have been presented with both the opportunities to learn treatment approaches beyond what I learned in traditional medical school as well as the circumstances to apply them. This has afforded me the opportunity to see the results first hand of putting several different views of reality into action. This book is an attempt to explain the approaches that I have found most capable of producing results that are gentle, powerful, reproducible and curative. For most Americans, this will represent a completely different explanation as to why your state of health contains a particular set of symptoms at any time. This reality will encompass the perspective of western medicine, traditional Chinese medicine and homeopathic medicine.

Mrs. B's case helps illustrate how life will bring you all you can handle, plus just a little bit more. Mrs. B had been a patient of mine for many years due to her disabling arthritis. She had first come to see me at age 75 years with painful arthritis of both knees. She was becoming progressively disabled and was unable to continue taking care of herself and her home. The X-rays of her knees showed extensive arthritis. Her family doctor had prescribed the usual medications but they didn't help much and they tended to upset her stomach. After presenting her with all of the options, her choice basically came down to having surgery or losing her independence. She chose surgery.

I took Mrs. B into surgery and replaced her left knee with an artificial knee. It was a wonderful success. Her pain was greatly relieved. Her range of motion and strength quickly returned to the leg. She was quite satisfied and soon was able to walk and take care of her house again. She was a quite stoic individual and was happy now that she had one good knee to support her. She was content to just tolerate the remaining disability from her other bad knee.

I saw Mrs. B once a year to check her X-rays and knee function. She continued to do well and was happy with her life of having one good leg to rely upon and one bad leg that she could favor. Since I live and work in a relatively small town, Mrs. B had heard through the local rumor mill that I was considering retiring from surgery and doing this strange "energy medicine" full time. This brought her back in about seven years after her first knee surgery to get the other one fixed. She was "getting tired of dragging this one bum knee around" and wanted it fixed before I retired from doing surgery. Her knee was quite stiff and swollen. Her X-rays were certainly terrible looking with big spurs all around the joint and no cartilage left in the joint space.

Since I had not planned to stop doing surgery for several months yet, we had time to try something else. She agreed as surgery was not her favorite thing to do. Mrs. B was given a homeopathic remedy, selected for her individual symptoms, and told to return in one month. Well, she was quite a sight to see in one month. She had lost 10 pounds from being able to walk as much as she wanted. She didn't sit around as much grumbling about old age and her complaints. This new outlook corresponded to a greatly improved function on her knee. It still had big bony spurs and stiffness, but the swelling and tenderness was greatly reduced. After three months had passed, there was hardly any pain at all. It felt as comfortable to her as the artificial knee.

I have followed Mrs. B for several years now and she continues to do well and is quite satisfied with her treatment. Mrs. B would have no reason to deceive me, so I have to assume her reports of minimal pain and a feeling of well-being are the truth. But it shouldn't be possible! At least according to what I had learned in medical school. The only changes in her therapy were the addition of a homeopathic remedy and she stopped taking her anti-inflammatory medication. Her X-rays still showed the pattern of someone with severe arthritis.

What had happened to all the "truth and reality" that I had originally leaned in medical school and orthopedic residency? In order to understand this new reality, it will be best to take it one step at a time and build up a stable foundation of understanding.

It seems almost automatic that after I give a presentation on the alternative treatment of various medical conditions, I will be asked the same question. How did I get interested in energetic medicine? I hope my story may help you, the reader, find your own path, to get the most out of your life, and enjoy your optimal state of health.

I would recommend focusing mainly on the **process** of discovery. Each one of you will have your own individual set of characteristics and life circumstances. Comparing examples from my life and the patients in my medical practice will help you see the range of possibilities. Life will bring you unique experiences and offer you the opportunity to make your own choices. You will see that each decision you make will have its own set of consequences.

I studied and practiced orthopedic surgery from 1973 to 2003. Orthopedics is a profession that reinforces a concrete definition of reality. The actions of a surgeon in the operation room must be based on a clear perception of the reality of his patient's condition. Surgery is not a place for doubt about the appropriateness of the intended procedure or the best steps to accomplish it. It is necessary for the surgeon to be quite sure of his plan to deal with his patient's condition. The plan should have a clear expectation of improving their life.

To make a change in how you approach treatment takes a lot of time and concerted effort. You will have to overcome your zone of comfort and familiarity. To gain comfort with a new concept of treatment requires investing the time necessary to learn its history and the accepted reasons why it is effective. It is desirable to pick the initial cases for its application where there is very little likelihood of doing any harm.

It takes a lot of patients like Mrs. B to overcome the indoctrination of traditional, American medicine. For me, it took the experiences of many hundreds of patients over several years of the combined practice of traditional orthopedics and complementary therapies.

Be patient with yourself and your doctors as you gain knowledge and experiences with these "alternative" realities. It is good to approach this learning process with an *open mind* and *flexibility*. Keeping a *balance* between your previous "truths" and the new "truths" is recommended. You may make faster progress with less difficulty if you see the new as being added to the old, rather than replacing or deleting your former understandings.

In the 1980's, I was practicing orthopedic surgery at a community hospital in Ohio. The hospital hired a new anesthesiologist who was trained in traditional Chinese medicine. We spent many hours working together in surgery and he introduced me to the concepts of Chinese medical theory. After being in practice for a few years, all surgeons will have some cases that are just not curable or responsive to any therapies. In orthopedics, most of these patients will be people suffering with chronic pain that can only be made tolerable by taking medications. I tested his theories by sending him the most resistant cases for treatments. Lo and behold, many of these patients were significantly relieved of their pain. Many of the patients, that I previously had no way to help, were now getting relief without surgery or drugs.

Now what was I to think of that? I had applied all that I had learned in traditional orthopedics to these patients to little avail. He could stick a few needles in them and over time they stopped complaining and needed less medicine.

When confronted with this situation, I often see doctor's reacting in one of several ways. They may think that their treatment just finally took hold and really helped the patient. They may think the patient was just malingering all along and was faking the symptoms. The doctor may think the patient stopped complaining because he didn't want to be stuck with any more needles. The recovery commonly may be dismissed as just some "placebo effect" or a "spontaneous remission", without any further consideration of what may have really happened.

The most challenging explanation may be that this system of energetic medicine of the Chinese is valid and equal to our western system of medicine. If that is true, how come it was never mentioned in medical school or anywhere else in the orthopedic literature of the 1980's?

Since I had selected out the patients for referral, and knew their cases before and after acupuncture, it was hard to admit that there was any likely explanation besides the fact that Chinese medicine was a valid approach to treatment. Since I was born with a condition that I might diagnose as "terminal curiosity", I chose to study the principles and practice of Chinese medicine and experiment with offering it to my patients.

Practicing acupuncture in the office gave me the opportunity to observe the results first hand. I would recommend keeping some balance between the traits of curiosity and courage with the traits of patience and respect for what has been established as the norm. I would advise you to move forward with new realities in a way that adds value to yourself and those who come into contact with you. All new knowledge and skills have a learning curve associated with it. Even in expert hands all treatments have something less than 100% effectiveness or assurance of an optimal result.

Having been previously trained in western medicine is of almost no help in understanding the concepts of Chinese medicine. There is a great deal of subtlety required in making a diagnosis in the Chinese system of medicine. The measurements of the state of energy and health in the patient are quite subjective. For example, very subtle differences in the feel of the pulse at the wrist will indicate the source and location of a patient's symptoms.

The Chinese system of medicine was established long before the tools of laboratory medicine were available. The doctor needs to be able to observe and understand the "energetic state" of the patient to make a diagnosis or treatment recommendation. The patient's energy must be observed or felt in the superficial tissues of the body. The findings seen on the surface of the body will relate to conditions on the interior of the body.

The Chinese have had for centuries an understanding of the human being as being a holographic body. All functions of the body are understood to be represented in each smaller part. Palmistry, iridology and reflexology were understood in Chinese medicine long before it was recognized in the west. Chinese medicine makes use of very subtle changes on the surface of the body to make diagnoses and treatment decisions. I found the subjectivity of the evaluation methods quite confounding. They were difficult to learn as quickly as I would have liked. They seemed to fit the Chinese temperament better than my American impatience and perfectionism.

For this reason, I was attracted to electro-acupuncture which allows you to do a quantitative measurement of each of the body's meridians (lines of energetic communication in the body). Once the acupuncture points were learned and the technique of measurement was practiced, a reproducible measurement of the patient's energy state could be obtained. Having an objective measurement of electrical resistance on the skin was more in the frame of reference of what I was used to. It was quite similar to measuring the energy of the heart (EKG) or brain (EEG). I was familiar with these type of measurements of the body's energy system as valid measures of physiology and therefore sought out people who were working with these systems and completed training in their use.

One of the first patients I treated with electro-acupuncture was as impressive as Mrs. B. I was quickly hooked on it and pursued more of the possibilities. This patient was a middle aged woman with rheumatoid arthritis of about three years duration. She had an aggressive disease process that was not well controlled on prednisone, methotrexate and plaquanil. After a few months of electro-acupuncture, she recovered completely without any evidence of the disease in her joints or on the blood tests. This was almost 15 years ago and she has continued to stay well without any further treatment or need of medications. Everything I had learned prior to this time said that this was not possible, but I had now seen it happen.

Based upon these results, I researched further and studied the work of Dr. Voll. He had developed a sophisticated system of diagnostic and therapeutic electro-acupuncture in Germany over the last 25 years. The logic of the science was quite advanced and the anatomical elegance of the energetic system of the body was precisely detailed. It had al the parameters that define a medical study as a science: measurability, reproducibility, predictability and verifiability.

Studying the German system of electro-acupuncture presented a whole new dilemma and challenge. Dr. Voll had found in treating patients, and the abnormalities he measured in their energetic system, that while electro-acupuncture was more accurate in making a diagnosis the patients corrected their abnormal energetic findings and healed even better when they were treated with homeopathic remedies.

Dr. Voll found the results of homeopathic treatment were more powerful than either acupuncture or western medicine. Dr. Voll was trained in both traditional Chinese medicine and western medicine but was familiar with homeopathic medicine as it originated in Germany and remained common there.

Now this was a little discouraging. I wondered how it could be that there is a medical science, completely unknown to me, that is even more effective than what I had spent the last 20 years studying?

Being an optimist at heart, I thought "OK, I will just take a look". Up until that point, homeopathy seemed to be totally implausible. It seemed beyond logic that it could be anything besides a fairy tale. Treatment solutions were used in homeopathy that contained nothing more than water. Ten years later, I have to agree with Dr. Voll. This is the most powerful treatment system I have yet found. This is especially true in chronic diseases. I have now been fortunate to learn how the homeopathic system works and see the amazing results that it can deliver.

Being "terminally curious", I have looked at many other alternative systems. This included completing training programs in hypnosis, neurotherapy (EEG biofeedback), NAET (Nambudripad's allergy elimination technique), Reiki, craniosacral therapy, computer assisted quantitative vocal analysis and therapy and many other less common therapies. They may all have an appropriate place in the treatment of symptoms, but none seem to have the universal application and effectiveness of homeopathy. After all of this, I have dedicated myself the last eight years to the study of homeopathic medicine and integrating it with the other modalities.

My long process of discovery has only been possible due to the tolerance and support of my family and patients. I often tell patients that I truly may be the most boring person they ever meet. I watch very little television or some of the common things others are doing. I enjoy learning new things. I have been in school so many years it is ridiculous. But that is what I enjoy. So, now I am going to focus here on the principles that can bring you closer to the end point of understanding healing much faster than I got there.

My path of study is only pertinent to who I am and the life circumstances that have been presented to me. It would not be appropriate or advisable for anyone else to try and trace my career through medical education. Your correct path is yours only. It will be there for you if you look for it. You likely do not need to know some of the things I have learned. I likely do not need to know all the things you know. You need to find what is helpful for you to accomplish the goals that are part of your life. We exist in the same world, though. Therefore, the basic principles and process presented in this book will apply in some way to your experiences of health or disease in this lifetime.

For your reference on the incalculable amount of information that is available, visit a library. Notice the enormous number of books there (joke). Each book contains the experiences or knowledge that someone has gained in their lifetime. They have written it down for our benefit. No one person could know it all or needs to know it all. We need to learn what best suits our individual purpose in life and learn that well. Again, the emphasis should be on the process of learning as much as the information gained.

Over the last 30 years there has been a huge increase in the amount of information available in medicine. This is driven both by the academic world's desire to do research and the nature of the business of medicine. "Publish or perish" is important to maintain status and income in the academic world. To be commercially viable, you may have to "one up" the field and gain a competitive advantage. This puts greater information in the hands of physicians and patients, which gives a heightened sense of security and the impression that we know exactly what we are doing. This serves the dual purpose of allowing the patient and the surgeon to sleep well at night thinking all is known and will go well.

Unfortunately, critically reading the scientific literature in medicine may be enlightening. No drug is 100% effective for all cases in which it is indicated or without any side effects. No surgery has complete reliability or certainty of producing normal function. Very few diseases have been conquered in that they are completely cured or prevented. Great debates go on among ideological camps in medicine that are equally committed to competing and opposite approaches to therapy.

Weight loss programs are a good example of how little consensus there is among the medical profession in an area that has been studied and been with us forever. The number of diet plans available to us is quite extensive and the results are terrible. Long term follow up studies show that 95% of people put on a diet by a physician will end up gaining weight in the long run. Look around, how many overweight physicians have you encountered? Obviously, we are not holding back some secret. If there was one understanding and one treatment, there wouldn't be shelves of competing books, available for your purchase with each one claiming to have the answer.

The number of examples of this lack of consensus in medicine can go on and on. Look at the strikingly different options presented for heart disease, breast cancer, arthritis, ulcerative colitis or any number of conditions. Each disease has its proponents for surgery and its proponents for drug management. In all these areas, the research has been extensive for decades and still there is no consensus.

With this "realistic" background, you can now approach the second question for this chapter. Again, keep an open mind when considering if it is reasonable to question the validity of your grasp on reality. There are other perspectives of reality you have yet to discover. Adding new perspectives to your knowledge base will bring you closer to seeing the "true reality".

Second question: who and what will you blame (or give credit to) for causing your symptoms—and who or what does your doctor blame? Now, why does this question matter? Does its answer only have value in assigning blame, or can an investigation into the processes of making this decision influence your state of your health?

My experiences would lead me to say that yes, your physical health will be determined by and closely linked with your state of mind and emotions. This holistic understanding of health is likely the most important change in your perspective that reading this book can offer you. All of the science and evidence of the subsequent chapters are designed to lay the ground work for your growth in understanding. You are then free to draw your own conclusions when you add this information to what you have previously learned. You will want to verify the validity of this information by applying it to every day situations in your life. For a principle to approach the level of truth it must meet the same criteria as does any science (measurability, predictability, verifiability and reproducibility).

In looking at the question of whom or what is determining your health, the first thing that is helpful to do is move far away from assigning blame or guilt. These emotions will give too much charge to the question of what is causing your symptoms and limit how open your mind can be. A calmer head and heart will allow you to examine the cause of your symptoms and be open to things that you are just not able to see now.

With a closed mind, you will likely find it is more comfortable to stand pat on what you already think or judge to be the truth. If the case is that everything is perfect in your life in every way, this would probably be a good choice. But if there is a situation in your life that could use improving, learning some new tools to move out of the place where you are now stuck and get "unstuck" is a good choice. As you move through the concepts presented in this book, you should attempt to gain some new tools that make if far easier to discard old habits of blame and guilt.

What is being presented is in its essence a method of evaluating your awareness. Your awareness and your perspective are closely linked. In a similar way your familiarity and comfort are linked. Familiarity and comfort are both a result of your awareness. Even if an influence in your life is not what you would want it to be, you will have a level of comfort with it just because it is familiar. Inversely, those things that you have no awareness of will not have this level of comfort. Developing a level of comfort with the alternative options available in treating and preventing symptoms requires just this challenge of expanding your awareness.

For this change in awareness to occur, one needs a considerable amount of four skills:

1. A willingness to be open minded
2. Honesty in appraising your current level of health and its causes
3. Persistence in applying new principles
4. Objectivity in evaluating the results of old and new treatment options

You only need to learn a new process of evaluating the results of your treatment options for these skills to become more useful and automatic in your approach to improving your health and enjoyment in life. Keep these goals in mind as you proceed. You will be presented with the steps necessary to accomplish these goals and given examples of their use in recovering or maintaining good health.

It may help to remember the example of the public library in assessing just how much you really know. My impression is that it takes an attitude of humility to be able to see and deeply take in new sweeping concepts that have important implications for your state of health. I know from a surgeon's perspective, it took a long time for me to learn enough that I became aware of how little I really knew. This is the "arrogance of ignorance"—not an easy thing to correct.

Before this first chapter ends, I want to give you one more question to work on as you proceed through the rest of the chapters and their concepts. That question is: **where do your ideas come from?**

Certainly in neuro-anatomy we have never located any part of the physical brain that has the ability to create an original idea. There is also no physical location in the brain for the concept that we call our mind. So, when you have an original thought, (one that you never heard before or read anywhere), (one that you gladly take credit for without knowing how or why it came to you), (one that may be consistent with the other information contained in your data bank of conscious knowledge, but has never previously occurred to you as a result of that knowledge), where did that original thought come from?

Who or what entity deserves the credit as the creative information bank that you can tap into for new ideas that can benefit you or others. I don't have a definite answer for this question anymore than you do. But, I can give you some reproducible observation on the process. That is, that the less you take credit for these ideas and the more you see them as a gift to you, the more often you will receive these gifts and benefit from their impact on your life.

Your Healing Heart

AWARENESS

All Healing is Self-Healing

Law of Similars =
The Healing Law of Nature

Healing = Transforming
Susceptibility into Resistance

Vital Force = "The Big You"

The Disease of Fear

ACCEPTANCE

Changing Your Perception of Reality

Being Open-Minded to
Alternative Views of Reality

It's OK to Talk to Yourself
and Listen to Your Body

The Amazing Human Being

Western Medicine has Value
as a Healing System

FORGIVENESS

The Meaning of Symptoms and Disease

You're OK

Healing: The Never Ending Story
= Learning and Healing Through
Life's Opportunities and Challenges

Chapter 2

All Healing Is Self-Healing

Once you grasp the optimism and exciting potential that comes with the awareness that all healing is ultimately self-healing, you will have taken the first steps towards enjoying good health. In this chapter you will be presented with the full implications of self-healing. "All healing is self-healing" is a phrase commonly encountered in the world of holistic and energetic medicine. The daily practice of homeopathic medicine confirms the truth of this principle and allows you to see and feel first hand the process of self-healing.

Once you have experienced healing yourself and know it to be a reality after using homeopathic remedies, you can also observe the same healing principle to be acting in other healing systems. The utilization of your natural ability to heal is recognized in a number of holistic health care systems and represents the basis of their therapy. Both homeopathic medicine and traditional Chinese medicine have utilized the principle of self-healing consistently in patients for centuries.

Due to the fundamental truth of the phenomenon that self-healing is always your mechanism of true healing; many other more modern treatments also utilize the same principle without their even being aware of it. We will take a look at these other systems in order to have a thorough understanding of the practical application of the concept of all healing as self-healing.

It may be necessary to first define the word healing. A definition of healing that represents true or complete healing should include both the removal from the patient of all suffering as symptoms as well as the removal of whatever limitations they were experiencing in their ability to enjoy life. When you heal through self-healing, it will be holistic and result in a lessening of the probability of the recurrence in the future of the original symptoms. Holistic healing can affect your past, present and future state of health. It is important in comparing the results of your various treatment options to limit your concept of healing to this definition.

Healing is a different phenomenon than personal growth or development. It would not be an appropriate use of the word healing to include attempts to achieve some state of "super" functioning. The goal of healing does not go beyond the normal or natural capabilities you are given as a unique human being. For example, no matter how hard I tried as a youth, I could never jump high enough to dunk a basketball. A system of therapy whose purpose is healing would not have a goal for me that included dunking a basketball. This could be a goal of healing only if I had previously been able to dunk a basketball and had lost that ability due to an illness or injury.

Symptoms that are associated with aging or a state of health that causes no symptoms would also not need "healing". By definition, a desire to change your eye color from brown to blue would not be a healing process. Aging and the specific limitations you have in your capabilities are your individual and natural, genetic expressions. They are a normal expression and not a disease state. Healing represents a normal and natural process of recovering your inherent potential for good health.

To have a complete grasp of the *process of healing,* you will want to study the implications of the various mechanisms you can choose for treating symptoms. Specifically, you want to learn why different types of therapy get the results that are commonly seen with them. In addition, you should learn what the different quality of results obtained with different systems of treatment can teach you in terms of the healing process.

You usually are presented with several alternative choices for treatment when a new symptoms presents. In making your choice of treatment from among the options, you will be best served by being able to anticipate what the short and long term implications of the treatment will be. *The most important goal is to be able to determine if the chosen therapy is just dealing with symptoms or is treating the cause of the symptoms.* Symptoms will be demonstrated to always be only the effects of some other underlying cause. A purely symptomatic treatment may leave the underlying cause unchanged. Your more ideal choice for therapy will deal with the symptoms by treating their cause.

Health is the goal of healing. Health involves comfort on all levels: the physical level as well as the mental-emotional level. It is often demonstrated in holistic medicine that for a state of good health to be present, it must be good simultaneously on all levels. For example, your level of physical health will have a close correspondence to your mental and emotional state of health. Good health is your goal and should be your natural state. This opinion is based on both how you usually begin life and the possibilities of recovering good health that you are about to see demonstrated.

The statement "All healing is self-healing" should be understood to be a source of optimism. I would like to spend some time on a number of examples that demonstrate the reality of self-healing. Having optimism for your potential to heal will be easier once you learn the practical application of the concept of self-healing and its demonstrated potential. I will start by highlighting the implications of your potential for self-healing, so that you can then keep these implications in mind as you explore the following examples.

An important principle inherent in the concept of self-healing is that you *always* have within you the capability to heal. Let's review some examples intended to demonstrate that the amazing capability you have to heal is **equal** to your capability to produce symptoms.

This normal, human capacity for healing is greatly under appreciated and under utilized in western medicine. I am quite sure I never heard this concept emphasized in medial school.

The emphasis was more on learning the processes of disease than the healing process.

Somehow, in medical school we studied normal anatomy and physiology but never really spent much time studying healing. The training was primarily based in the philosophy that disease represents a malfunctioning of the body. Therefore, treatments were designed to remove the disease by working against the body's ability to produce the symptoms of the disease. Symptoms were understood to be the manifestations of a disease process. My training was to overpower these manifestations of the body (symptoms) with either surgery or drugs. Since the symptoms were seen as errors or problems instead of the corrective or healing efforts of the body, it was then quite appropriate to work against them or "anti" (as in antihistamines, anti-inflammatories, antibiotics or antifebrile agents).

You must clearly recognize that this philosophy of intentionally working against the body has completely contrasting goals and results when compared with the holistic systems of medicine that have the intention of working with the body. Holistic and energetic systems of medicine recognize symptoms as having an entirely different purpose. *The body is always assumed to be attempting to heal itself. The symptoms are understood to represent the efforts made by the body to heal.* Get ready for a radical change in your perspective. In chapter three you will be presented with the strikingly opposite view of symptoms, that at the level of their purpose, *symptoms will be understood to be good things.*

This alternative view of the meaning of symptoms is such a fundamental difference, that very little else of the information in this book will make sense, until you are able to see a clear difference between these two approaches to understanding and treating symptoms. Once this difference is clearly seen and kept in mind in evaluating the methods used in a treatment, you will have no trouble recognizing at any time the type of treatment you are choosing.

This different interpretation of the meaning of symptoms with your recognition that all healing is self-healing contains the essence of your expanded opportunity to improve your health. As you learn the principles of holistic medicine, you should recognize that you have the ability to heal, that you are always attempting to heal and that by working with your body's attempts to heal you can achieve the highest quality result.

What I am encouraging you to do is to become more informed. Putting this knowledge to work can give you confidence and a rational basis for making decisions on how to treat whatever symptoms you experience. The better informed you are, the better chance you have of making the best choices. You will also be better armed to avoid choices that would not be in the best interests of your health. At the least, it will allow you to ask better questions of others and yourself. It comes down to the choice between being passive and just letting things be done to you because that is what is expected or being pro-active in the face of unfamiliar decisions.

It is easy to be overwhelmed by the complexity of medical language and be influenced by the automatic assumption that you have to defer your ability to make a decision to the recommendations of "experts". Unless you can ask a reasonably informed question, it may be quite hard to find out how expert their opinion really is. My experience is that often the more critical is the decision you are facing, the more you will be afraid to ask questions. When you receive a shock of bad news about your health, you will often go into a state of "shock" and not think or act as rationally as other times. Knowing that **you** are controlling the process of self-healing helps put you more in charge of choosing how you contract with others to assist in your healing.

Along with being optimistic, the concept of self-healing has inherent implications for accepting personal responsibility for your state of health. As you further examine the healing process, it will offer you a window of opportunity to see the importance of factors controlling your health from two entirely different views.

Are you the victims of circumstances beyond your control, or are you really the captains of your own fate and actually determining your state of health? We will look at experiences that shed some light on where the balance of proof lies between these two options. Applying the principles of science (predictability, etc.), should shed some light on this question. I will present information to take your examination of healing beyond just philosophy and add some measure of science.

People often ask if homeopathy isn't just a placebo effect. My experience is consistent with two centuries of homeopathic medicine and leads me to the conclusion that it is not placebo effect but a far different type of healing. The placebo phenomenon, though, makes a great starting point for a discussion of healing and self-healing.

The reality of the placebo effect is recognized as a valid concept by almost everyone. In most medical trials the placebo effect will result in 20% to 30% of the "untreated" group receiving the intended benefits of the therapy. Often, the effectiveness of the drug or therapy being evaluated will not be 30% greater than the placebo effect (or 60% total effect). In some medical experiments the placebo effect ends up being greater than the therapeutic effect of the drug that is being tested.

The placebo response is quite universal. What can be learned from this universal healing response? It shows up in all experiments and can even be a negative or a positive response depending upon the experimenter's design. The placebo healing response results from the expectation or perceived intention that healing will result from an experimental trial.

The healing result that is called a placebo response occurs entirely as a self-healing phenomenon. The placebo response is produced by subjects that were randomly chosen to receive a sham therapy. It seems quite logical to conclude from the demonstrated reality of the placebo effect that the human being has the potential to heal itself by its own innate abilities. This healing potential applies to all experiments and all diseases that we potentially encounter. This alone is quite a startling revelation.

The reality of the power and universal application of the placebo self-healing phenomenon is surely a source of optimism. Not only is all healing ultimately self healing but there are no limitations on the symptoms or diseases to which it may apply. Medical trials are often short term and therefore do not determine how permanent a placebo form of healing has the potential to be. To help us answer the question of how long can self-healing last, there is a great deal of evidence available about the human potential for long term self-healing in recorded cases of spontaneous remission.

Spontaneous remissions, by definition, are cases where patients have completely recovered normal health for a long period of time, without receiving any form of therapy or where the treatment used was considered to be unlikely to have any effect. The knowledge in this area has been greatly assisted by two authors, Brendan O'Regan and Caryle Hirshberg. They researched well documented cases of spontaneous remission that were published in the modern medical literature. They only included cases from respected, peer-reviewed medical journals. Their book "Spontaneous Remission An Annotated Bibliography" is a collection of these publications and contains an extensive variety of cases with all types of disease (congenital abnormalities, tumors, metabolic diseases, cancers and infections).

The wide variety of diseases contained in the case reports is surprising because this is not an area where there has been much interest in publishing case reports. I would guess that the majority of spontaneous remissions never get published in the medical literature as they are too perplexing for the medically trained investigator.

The author's second work "Remarkable Recoveries" is a much more detailed accounting of the experience of a large number of terminal cancer patients who had complete remissions of their disease. Again, these patients recovered without traditional medical intervention. Both the placebo effect and cases of spontaneous remission help define the possibilities for self-healing and document the reality of these capabilities. Some of the cases are so fantastic as to seem unbelievable, but they have been scrupulously documented and followed up for years.

In order to learn the nature of the healing phenomenon, it seems most advisable to study the processes that have demonstrated this remarkable success. Medical researchers should all be looking at these self-healing processes and fundamentally re-evaluate the principles and judgments they are using in designing their research. The placebo response and spontaneous remissions should stimulate them to reassess the assumptions they are making about the healing process. The emphasis should be on the process of healing. At the very least, the process of self-healing demands further examination as it causes no side effects and has very little expense associated with it.

The study of self-healing will set the stage for your study of healing in this book. The main question is how do treatments become curative by holistic standards. How do some treatments address the underlying cause of a disease and trigger this self-healing mechanism? These types of treatment appear to not just deal with symptoms as a secondary manifestation of the disease but treat the underlying cause of the disease.

It will be helpful to follow a logical sequence in evaluating the healing process in your attempts to maintain and recover good health. First, the principles and the steps necessary for triggering the healing process should be consistent. Then, evaluating whether a treatment acts according to the principle of all healing is self-healing needs to meet the criterion of being a science. It is then appropriate to study the mechanism of self-healing. Next, the universal ability of healing needs to be demonstrated to be a consistent reality (placebo and spontaneous remissions should be consistent with using Chinese medicine or homeopathic remedies).

After the reality of self-healing is established, your study can then advance to evaluating the known processes that can be called into action to trigger the self-healing process. You will want to compare the quality of the results that each available process can produce in the short and long term. The next step will be to understand how these processes work and why they are able to produce the type of results that are associated with them.

Understanding the results you see from the interaction between your self-healing mechanism and the type of therapy you have chosen to use is *the key to discovering the cause of your state of health.* When you are able to get to this level of awareness, (knowing of the cause of your symptoms), several positive benefits become available. This level of understanding will more likely guarantee that the results of your therapy will be permanent and that the outcome will be as close as possible to your best potential health. You will then have the information you need to choose a treatment that will work powerfully and not create any side effects.

Once you are able to know the underlying cause for any disease you are experiencing (defined as a particular set of symptoms), you will have another important choice to make. That choice will be: what is the best treatment for your disease. The information you are being presented with in this book will give you a basis for making the choice of whether to choose to work against yourself or with yourself. There will always be many other factors to consider in making a decision on what type of treatment is best for you. There are other factors such as the urgency of the situation and the knowledge and the resources available to you at the time when a decision has to be made. The relative importance of these factors may dictate either choice as being the right one. The choice that you make will also be dependent upon your knowledge of the facts and your prejudices towards them.

There can be many reasons for choosing to work against yourself in the face of chronic disease. It may be the only option that you are aware of. You may choose treatments that work against yourself as a result of holding a negative, unconscious opinion about yourself. If you see yourself as being worthy of blame or suffering, symptoms may be a retaliation for your present thoughts about yourself or your past actions. A negative state of mind like guilt can be silently behind the persistence of your symptoms in a chronic disease.

When you choose to work with yourself, it is more likely that you will see yourself as worthy of healing. This state of mind is more consistent with the principles and approach of energetic, holistic medicine. The symptoms you are producing will be understood to be the most beneficial healing response to a challenging event occurring in your life. The adverse events in your life are understood to be offering you the potential for healing as a process of strengthening yourself through overcoming challenges. Life's challenges can be seen as a maturing or evolutionary process instead of something purely negative and tending to overwhelm you.

The alternative choices of working with or against your symptoms bring consequences that are radically different. Before you can be certain of your preferences for healing with or against yourself, you need to evaluate how and why you establish your preference. You can then consistently choose in a way that provides curative healing. Your investigation into healing should look at why you make the conclusions you do about the cause of your problem. This is based upon seeing the cause and effect relationship between experiences and your reaction to them. This knowledge can be expanded as you make a variety of choices when faced with a symptomatic challenge and compare the results of making various choices. To save time and suffering, it will help to study medical history. This study can help you avoid less desirable choices that result in more unfavorable consequences.

As we study healing through looking at various healing systems, it is important to consider not only the *process* involved but also look for the *principles* behind the process. This will help you know if the treatment is dealing with the underlying cause of the disease or just its secondary symptoms.

Once the principles directing the self-healing process are known, your state of health should be recognized to be quite logical. The logic behind your state of health is best seen when life's events are viewed from a cause and effect standpoint. You should strive to see a logical time-line between challenging events in your life and your symptomatic response to them.

It will be helpful in your study of healing systems to investigate the exceptional patients—the remarkable recoveries—those patients that demonstrate exceptional healing without or despite any intervention from established medical practice. In "Remarkable Recoveries", the authors have attempted to group patients somewhat together by similar healing processes. Individual chapters tell of patients who made similar changes in their lives that were then followed by recovery of their health.

The placebo effect and spontaneous remissions together clearly point to the reality of the phenomenon of self-healing. To be able to generalize to *all* healing, it will be helpful to study the processes of healing in successful and universally applicable systems of healing. After studying a variety of systems of medicine, it appears that some come closer to this ideal than others. It is in making comparisons between the final results from healing with each of the alternative choices that the principles involved in healing are easier to see.

It will be helpful in evaluating apparently successful cases of healing to determine the quality and the permanence of their recovery. The chance of having a recurrence of the same symptom or disease following treatment gives an indication if the underlying cause of the disease has been treated with each type of therapy. To help illustrate some of these principles, I would like to use another case from my practice.

This case is a patient that came in shortly after I had make the decision to leave the specialty practice of traditional orthopedic surgery and practice holistic medicine. This case has helped teach me several important things, plus made me quite comfortable with the switch to a new type of medical practice. Cases like this may stimulate you to investigate your alternative choices for treating symptoms.

Bill was a patient in his sixties who could certainly be considered "terminal". He had the unlucky occurrence of two separate forms of cancer (bladder and prostate). Things were not going well for him in that the tumors were widely spread around the body in the lymph nodes, the liver and his lungs. Further treatment with chemotherapy or radiation did not have much hope to offer him. It was at this point that he considered holistic medicine as worth a try. He had no prior experience with it but was open minded enough to consider it. He recently had some large lymph nodes removed from his armpit that puzzled his doctors. Under the microscope they appeared to be metastatic melanoma (a malignant skin cancer). They went over his body carefully and could find no skin cancers.

Bill had an extensive workup with multiple scans showing metastatic disease through out the body. It was finally a PET scan that located the melanoma. It was located on the back of his tongue, where they had not been able to see it. It was biopsied and found to be the source of his melanoma. It was at this point that I saw him. The question at that time in his treatment was if the melanoma had spread across the diaphragm with liver and other lymph node involvement, there might not be any further treatment with a reasonable chance of helping him.

After spending several hours with Bill collecting all the data needed for a holistic approach to his treatment, he was begun on a sequence of homeopathic remedies according to the protocol of Dr. Ramakrishnan from Bombay, India. Dr. Ramakrishnan has reported good results in the treatment of over 5,000 patients with cancer.

Approximately six weeks after beginning treatment, Bill returned to the hospital for a CT guided biopsy of the lesions in his liver. This had been scheduled to determine if the lesions were from the melanoma or one of his other cancers. He ran into a problem during his biopsy. The lesion needed to be localized on the CT scan to be able to do a percutaneous needle biopsy. The doctors could not find the lesions in the liver anymore.

The oncologists were puzzled by this disappearance of the tumor and felt that in this circumstance, it would then be appropriate to remove his melanoma. Unfortunately, to adequately remove the melanoma, Bill would have to have a radical neck resection that entailed removal of the tongue and most of the right side of his mouth, jaw and soft tissues of the neck. He would have to have a tracheotomy and feeding tube. To the way of thinking of the oncologist and surgeon, this would be his best treatment and necessary according to the "standard of care".

Bill's surgery was scheduled for a few weeks later and he consulted me for a second opinion. I was encouraged by the "disappearance" of the liver metastasis, but not confident enough in what this might mean to recommend that he not have surgery. I told him I felt that there was a chance that the surgery might be excessive for his overall condition; it was somewhat risky and certainly painful at the least. Since he had cancer throughout the body, it seemed like an attempt to be "doing something" and would necessarily stop short of addressing his overall predisposition to cancer.

The rationale of removing the primary tumor to prevent the spread to other parts of the body was certainly one that had been well indoctrinated in my thought process up until this time in my medical studies. It was my reluctance to let go of this former mentality and approach to disease. That led me to tell Bill that I was not sure exactly what would be best for him. In that case, he chose to follow the advice of the "experts" at the cancer center.

Bill had his surgery scheduled about a week later. The surgery started at about three in the afternoon. I did not hear anything until the next day, when his wife called me to say that the surgery had been very difficult and he was in surgery until 1 o'clock in the morning. The surgeons had done sequential biopsies starting with the tongue to determine the extent of spread of his cancer. Each time they took a biopsy, the pathologist read the slides as showing no evidence of any cancer.

The surgeons continued to look and biopsy. No cancer. Their previous needle biopsy of the tongue had definitely showed malignant melanoma. Finally, after several hours, they had no where else to look and stopped taking biopsies. They repaired all the biopsies and reconstructed their work rather than remove his tongue and face. Bill had to have a tracheotomy for a few days, but recovered just fine.

How does a doctor feel when he gets a phone call like that? Talk about mixed emotions. As a surgeon myself, I know the traumatic procedure this patient has just gone through and that it was probably unnecessary. But then, here is a man who in a few months has completely healed "terminal cancer". Boy, did I realize that I still have a lot to learn. Well, we all do, so this is as good a time to start as any.

What is the nature of this self-healing process Bill had just demonstrated so dramatically before our eyes? It is two years later now and Bill continues to be in fine health and overjoyed with his new lease on life. He is one of a growing number of exceptional cases that I have now been privileged to witness heal themselves. It is worth your time to take a hard look at the question of why so many people experience exceptional recoveries of their health using homeopathic remedies.

Remember, all healing is self-healing. I am not healing the patients. My patients heal themselves. I try to teach them they can heal themselves and match them with the tools most helpful in the process of healing. But, what is the process? That is the point of writing this book—not having to teach one patient at a time. Learning more about the process of healing and its rules will give you the guidelines you need to heal. Learning a few new rules can make the healing results you obtain from the treatments you choose for your symptoms more certain and reproducible.

Very few of these cases get written up and reported in the western medical literature. Two hundred years of the published history of homeopathic medicine and thousands of years of traditional Chinese medicine exist where cases like these are reported. These cases are not included in "Spontaneous Remission". These cases are also not easily available for study by western physicians in the common literature resources they are exposed to.

American medical schools do a great job within their area of expertise. Their intentions to heal and serve are correct; they are just blinded, at the current time, to experiences outside their limited box of awareness. Paradoxically, my undergraduate school, Case Western Reserve University, and my medical school, Ohio State University, were homeopathic medical schools when they were originally founded. At the present time, that legacy has been driven so far out of their awareness, that it is hard to imagine how it can be recovered.

Why should we, the patients and the doctors, have to accept less in our choices for healing ourselves? This is particularly frustrating because the information about alternative medicine is available. This information is just not often in the minds or hands of those people in established positions of authority. It is quite difficult, at the present time, to get CME accreditation for alternative medicine meetings. This translates into a financial disincentive for physicians to include alternative approaches in the time they dedicate to continuing their education.

If you look back at Bill's case and the results of his treatment and ask yourself—could drugs and surgery have produced this result? Especially to have been successful with so little effort, so little cost and with no risk of any side effects. In the end, Bill ended up physically intact and stronger on all levels of his being. In my previous thirty years of experience with western medicine, this type of result or expectation of a result was hardly ever seen.

Conventional, western therapy with drugs and surgery certainly has a place in the options you should have available. You just need better information so you can be more realistic in your evaluation of the relative advantages and disadvantages of your various options. The actions of drugs and surgery take on a very different light in the reality of their "anti" nature. Their intention, by design, is to overpower the body's ability to produce a symptom. That is because symptoms are conceptualized to be the problem and not the answer to a problem.

Drugs or surgery may indeed be life saving at times. I would agree that they often are an appropriate first choice in the face of an acute medical problem. This is especially true, in the complete absence of a widespread understanding of the application of alternative approaches to acute medical crises, as is the current situation in the USA.

In an urgent situation, the first priority is to control the body's response and save both function and life. The American system of medicine excels at this. It is my opinion that where we have gone astray in our thinking is that we directly apply the approach that works well in an acute problems to the treatment of chronic conditions.

Before you throw too much cold water on western medicine, it is necessary to build up a better understanding of health and healing. It is not helpful just to point out the deficiencies of a drug and surgery based system of medicine without being able to offer a more rational and efficient alternative.

It is clearly true that in an acute medical emergency, drug therapy can be life saving. It may be a myth, though, that in chronic disease all that is need is more research and more powerful drugs in order to cure or control all diseases. In reality, has there ever been even one drug that was able to 100% of the time cure a disease?

Holistic medicine defines cure according to a very stringent standard. A curative treatment must meet several criterion to be considered as a full recovery:

1. That all symptoms of the disease are relieved
2. The patient has a decreased tendency for the symptoms to return
3. The patient is strengthened through treatment so that at the end of the recovery process no further drug is needed
4. In the treatment process no side effects are created

Under such a stringent standard for an ideal curative therapy, very few drugs will be found to meet these criteria. The primary reason for the failure of most drugs to meet this standard is in the site of action of the drug. To be curative, the drug must deal with the underlying cause of the condition. The drug will not be curative if it only treats the secondary symptoms of the disease. You must not confuse the symptoms with the cause of the disease.

It is important to recognize that diseases are experienced through symptoms but symptoms are not the underlying cause of a problem. To be curative, you must seek out the cause of the disease needing treatment. The secondary effects (symptoms) only represent the body's reaction to the underlying cause. This differentiation is crucial to understanding where the treatment you have chosen will be acting. With this knowledge you can predict the type of results each treatment can achieve.

Having a discussion of self-healing, cure and health is not in vain. There are many examples to study and learn from. I am optimistic for the future of medicine. It is possible to experience many positive benefits to your health just from having this discussion. One very nice result of understanding your health and symptoms, at this deep level, is that it frees you from blame and guilt. This freedom results from becoming aware of the cause of your symptoms. Being aware that your symptoms represent the body's response mechanism to some sort of stressful event is in itself the start of a healing process.

As we progressively begin to assemble the building blocks on which this theory of healing is based, you should feel empowered to take charge of your health. It can be a source of strength and optimism to know that there are systems available to you, which have successfully been able to assist healing for centuries. The more the public demands this approach to healing, the more the medical profession will respond.

The practice of medicine is a competitive situation in this country. Public demand has influence that may equal the powerful forces of the government, insurance industry and pharmaceutical companies. My bias is that the change needs to start with education. At the end of this book you may know many things that the faculty in our medical schools can't teach because they have never studied them. Their being unaware should not remain a defense any longer.

In the next several chapters you will be examining other questions that come to mind when considering the statement that all healing is self-healing. The focus will be on the meaning of your symptoms and the mechanism of healing. You are going to be presented with a very different view of the meaning of your symptoms. This view may turn your current understanding of the meaning of symptoms completely upside down.

Keep an open mind. Your growth in understanding requires taking a whole new look at symptoms. Are symptoms the problem or the answer in healing? It is common when a change in your perception is needed to just look harder at the small details of the current view you hold. Familiarity may influence your choices and patterns of thinking more than is wise. You can always go back to your old view. The knowledge gained from studying an alternative view of reality may even make your old views and understanding of reality more meaningful. If your existing views are correct, you should not fear their being challenged. If they are not correct, you should not fear their being corrected.

Your Healing Heart

AWARENESS

All Healing is Self-Healing

Law of Similars = The Healing Law of Nature

Healing = Transforming Susceptibility into Resistance

Vital Force = "The Big You"

The Disease of Fear

ACCEPTANCE

Changing Your Perception of Reality

Being Open-Minded to Alternative Views of Reality

It's OK to Talk to Yourself and Listen to Your Body

The Amazing Human Being

Western Medicine has Value as a Healing System

FORGIVENESS

The Meaning of Symptoms and Disease

You're OK

Healing: The Never Ending Story = Learning and Healing Through Life's Opportunities and Challenges

Chapter 3

The Healing Law of Nature—The Law of Similars

In this chapter you will be introduced to the "essence" of the healing mechanism that has been provided for your use as a universal principle of nature. At first, it may be helpful to review the definition of the term law of nature in the world of science. Defining the term law of nature helps you understand the Law of Similars as the healing law of nature. In science, a law of nature refers to a principle that is an absolute truth of our world. There will be no naturally occurring exceptions to a law of nature. Its truth is absolute and its actions are observed to be predictable, verifiable, reproducible and measurable. These laws of nature determine exactly how we will find the world to be.

Everyone is already familiar with the Law of Gravity as a law of nature. For our world to be as we know it, gravity has to always be acting in exactly the same way and with exactly the same force. Though gravity is an accepted fact of our world, the knowledge is not yet available to us why gravity exists or where the force of gravity comes from. The proof of gravity has to be in its existence and not in our ability to understand how or why it exists as a law of nature. For this reason, the Law of Gravity makes a nice analogy for the natural law of healing—Law of Similars.

The healing law of nature is called the Law of Similars. It has been known since ancient times. Hippocrates wrote of this healing phenomenon some 2500 years ago and it was used by him in his practice of medicine. Over all the years since then, there has never been an exception shown to the actions of the Law of Similars. The Law of Similars is just a reality of this world. It can only be observed as true by experience. The Law of Similars can only be known to exist as either having been created for your healing with the creation of the world or as having been brought into being by a mechanism as yet unknown. Current science and technology do not yet allow us to understand how this healing force is generated any more than we understand the force of gravity.

Though the appreciation of the Law of Similars as the healing principle of nature is quite ancient, it was not fully developed into a healing system until the late 1700's. The Law of Similars was formalized into a scientific system of medicine by Dr. Samuel Hahnemann. Over a period of about fifty years, he perfected the homeopathic system of medicine based on the Law of Similars. This system has not needed to make any fundamental changes since that time. Dr. Hahnemann developed most of the healing principles that are covered in this chapter. He spelled them out for us in his book "The Organon".

The homeopathic principles of healing using the Law of Similars have been tested and found to be accurate for over 200 years. Homeopathy was much more common in nineteenth century America than it is now. Homeopathy is currently a very large system of medicine world wide, but almost unknown in the USA. Many families have started to learn this system for themselves, in the face of a lack of trained professional practitioners. Fortunately, it lends itself to self-diagnosis and self-treatment quite readily.

Homeopathy presents such a different concept of healing from western medicine that in order to understand homeopathic healing you will need to thoroughly investigate its principles. The concept of like curing like is completely foreign to the concept of healing in modern American medicine. The Law of similars can be applied successfully without a full understanding of how it works but by understanding its principles of healing you can practice good preventative medicine.

Studying all of homeopathy's concepts in detail will help us understand, through comparison to western medicine, how these totally different systems of medicine can both produce a change in health. This study affords you an opportunity to increase your options for healing and potentially achieve a profoundly superior result.

The Law of Similars is translated into a working theory by only three words: **like cures like.** Like curing like can be translated as a defined property of the interaction of the materials of our world with the human being. *Every substance in the world possesses its own inherent and unique healing properties. All individual substance will have an equal ability to cure the identical symptoms that it has the ability to cause.*

The unique symptoms that a substance will be able to cause (and cure) have been found by giving it to a group of people and noting the reactions that are produced and specific to that substance. The substances used in homeopathic healing can be potentially anything found in the world. The types of symptoms a substance will produce are a unique property of that substance. The reaction produced by the substance being tested will not depend upon any individual characteristic of the person receiving the substance as part of their make-up or their individual state of health.

One of the initial accomplishments of Dr. Hahnemann was to define exactly what symptoms a variety of individual substance had the ability to produce when given to a group of healthy people. He did this by experimentation. Dr. Hahnemann experimented with the common substances used at the time in treating patients. People were given the substance, to be tested, repetitively until it produced symptoms. All new symptoms that were produced were recorded and then the trial was stopped. The new symptoms would leave after stopping the trial, and the person would return to their normal state of health. The trial was then repeated two more times in exactly the same manner. He wanted to be sure the symptoms were from giving the substance and not the result of something else occurring in the person's life.

Dr. Hahnemann found that each individual substance tested had the ability to cause a distinct set of symptoms when given to a group of healthy people. The homeopathic proving process has defined the actions of about 1000 substances quite well and around another 1000 substances only partially. These substances are mostly plants and minerals that were historically known to be active when used as a medicine. Only a small fraction of the potential substances in our world have been tested, so far, to find out what set of symptoms they can create or cure.

The common onion provides an easy to understand example of the application of the Law of Similars. Most people are familiar with the type of symptoms that will occur when chopping up onions. The following sequence of reactions will occur in virtually everyone during a prolonged exposure chopping onions. The first response to the onion is a stinging, burning sensation in the eyes followed by redness and tearing. The next symptoms produced by the onion will be a runny nose and sneezing. If you continue chopping onions a long time, you will find that as your nose runs, it tends to irritate and redden the upper lip, but the tears your eye produces will be bland and not redden the cheeks or area under the eye.

If you look at this picture of your symptomatic reaction to the onion, you can see why homeopaths commonly use the homeopathic remedy made from the onion to treat patients who complain of hay fever. The onion will relieve patients of their hay fever symptoms when the patient's symptoms closely match this set of symptoms. The added bonus is that when you treat the patient over a period of time with gradually more potent forms of the onion, he will not be susceptible to getting the symptoms of hay fever in future seasons. He will also not experience any new symptoms (side effects) like dryness or drowsiness commonly associated with the drug treatment of hay fever.

One of the many accomplishments of Dr. Hahnemann was his discovery of a pharmaceutical process where the curative properties of these substances could be maximized and the potential for any harmful effects minimized. The homeopathic pharmaceutical process produces a wide range of potencies for each substance, now called a remedy. This allows the strength of the healing reactions that the remedy can bring forward in the patient to be matched to his condition.

There are several goals in matching the patient with his ideal potency. The remedy will then be both gentle and rapid acting in the strength of the curative response it calls forth. The potency needs to be proportional to the severity of the symptoms and whether the patient's symptoms are acute or chronic in nature. The correct potency of the remedy will* act deeply to correct the underlying cause of the condition. The potency selected should be appropriate for how sensitive the patient is in his reactions. Finally, the potency of the remedy should allow for a permanent cure and strengthening of the patient's vitality to resist any future recurrences of the original symptoms.

One of the most obvious applications of the ability of the homeopathic pharmacy process to create both powerful and safe treatments for diseases is in the area of treating very serious or potentially fatal diseases. Remember the Law of Similars and treating like with like. In order to treat a serious disease like cancer, you may well be using a treating substance that in its natural form is a strong and potentially fatal poison. It is common for homeopaths treating seriously ill patients to use the homeopathic form of very toxic substances. Almost magically, after being prepared through dilution and succussion, these substances have no toxicity at all and can stimulate the self-healing process and the patient will recover good health.

A quite commonly used homeopathic remedy is made from arsenic. Arsenic demonstrates the principle of the Law of Similars nicely and the need for a pharmacy process that can turn deadly poisons into life savers. The clinical picture of a person acutely poisoned with arsenic is quite striking. They will die from shock secondary to fluid loss from protracted vomiting and diarrhea. They will have a mental picture alternating between complete lethargy and a state of restless agitation and fearfulness.

The process of dilution and succussion turns arsenic into a wonderful remedy to treat food poisoning or infectious gastroenteritis. I have had the opportunity to treat several patients with "Montezuma's revenge" acutely and see the startling results.

Anyone who has ever suffered from eating contaminated food or water can tell you that it is a miserable experience. Usually after taking a few doses of the 30C potency of arsenic, all the vomiting, diarrhea and cramping pain subsides and the patient can restfully sleep it off. The next day they feel quite well and are able to avoid that lingering feeling of toxicity and fatigue that can last for a few days. This is always a good remedy to have at home or when traveling.

It is quite important to note that homeopathic remedies do not have a "drugging" type of effect on the body. By design, the actions of a drug are to stop the body from producing a symptom. A drug is designed to interfere with one of the metabolic pathways of the body that is responsible for creating a symptom. Homeopathic remedies do not work to relieve symptoms by this mechanism. A homeopathic remedy can only work according to the Law of Similars.

A homeopathic remedy will only induce a healing response from the body. The remedy will not create new symptoms. A remedy adds energy to the body's existing symptoms. A remedy and a drug have the opposite type of action. If the person receiving the remedy does not have the same set of symptoms that the remedy has, the remedy will not have the ability to produce any reaction at all in this patient. This gives homeopathy its great advantage in safety. It will assist in healing only when the remedy is correctly matched to the patient's symptoms and if it is not the correct match for the symptoms, nothing will happen.

Be patient with the next few paragraphs. Some readers may need this dose of science to be comfortable with homeopathic pharmacy. Dr. Hahnemann found that through a process of repeated dilution and succussion, (a strong shaking of the solution), the healing properties of the original substance could be transferred to the diluted solution. He also found that the healing powers of the remedy could be altered in a way that gives them more ideal properties. The changes that take place in the remedy are specific and reproducible to the pharmacy process.

The results of this unique pharmacy process will at first glance seem to be illogical. That is, as the substance is progressively diluted and successed, it has the capability to induce a stronger and more rapid healing response. Experience shows that as the original substance becomes less from a material standpoint, and even non-material, it becomes progressively more potent in its actions.

The best understanding that I can offer you is that the healing capabilities of a substance on the body are not limited only to its properties as a material substance. Apparently, all substances exist simultaneously in both a material and an energetic state. This takes us into the difficult to conceptualize area of quantum physics.

Einstein's theory of relativity $\left(E = \frac{mc^2}{\sqrt{1 - v^2/c^2}}\right)$ can be translated to explain the phenomenon of homeopathic pharmacy. Our original substance (a material or m) exists in an identical (=) form as an energy (E). These two separate forms of the same substance are found in the practice of homeopathy to have an equal ability to heal symptoms but with different properties.

The homeopathic pharmaceutical process makes use of this energetic equivalent of the original material substance. This "quantum" nature of materials opens up a much greater range of usefulness for the healing substances of our world. It may be helpful to recall that a molecule of hydrogen, which we know of as part of the air we breathe, has an equal existence as a form of energy that was capable of blowing up the city of Hiroshima.

There are many profound implications that can be drawn from observing the process of recovering your health under homeopathic care. Try to keep these new principles in mind as you study the healing process. We are looking for the truth in the nature of healing and truth in the meaning of symptoms and disease.

A fascinating implication of homeopathic healing will seem counter-intuitive to what might be your expectations—especially if you fall more into the realist/pessimist category. The truth is that **when you give yourself more of the energy of your symptoms,** using an energetic homeopathic remedy (an energy that is the same as the energy of your symptoms—it is able to cause your symptoms when given to any healthy person), **you will *not*** suffer more; you will actually heal from those symptoms!

This fact at first glance can seem startling or illogical, but it can be proved to be true through experiemntation. The reality of this process is reproducible and predictable. It can be measured and verified. It fulfills all the criterion of being a science. Giving you more of the energy of your symptoms results in you healing yourself. Your whole understanding of the meaning of symptoms is about to change.

This form of healing (homeopathic) does not depend upon any factor besides the accuracy of the match between the patient's symptoms and the symptoms the remedy can cause. It does not matter who gives you the remedy or what pharmacy made the remedy. It does not even matter if you are a human or a horse. Homeopathic veterinarians find the Law of Similars applies to all animals just as well as it does to humans. This is not a system of belief. It is a scientific system of medicine that stimulates healing according to a universal Law of Nature.

The Law of Similars appears to be applicable to all symptoms and all diseases. There appears to be no exceptions to its actions as long as a similar remedy can be found. Both acute conditions and chronic diseases respond equally well to treatment. Not all homeopathic treatment is 100% effective, though. The healing principle may be absolute but homeopaths and patients will be less than perfect in the process of finding the similar remedy.

It is a daunting task to know the specific symptoms of 2000 remedies in order to find the closest match to the patient's symptoms. It is also often difficult for patients to relate their symptoms accurately to the homeopath. The success of treatment depends greatly on these two factors. Unfortunately, homeopathic training and experience in the USA has been severely limited for most of the last century.

Another important awareness that observing homeopathic healing affords you would be the reinforcement of *the holistic nature of the human being.* Your holistic nature becomes especially obvious in taking the case history from a patient with a chronic disease. The homeopathic history includes collecting the entire unique set of symptoms that make up each individual patient's experience of life.

The most powerfully curative remedy will be the one that best matches all the diseases that have come into the patient's life. If you can find a matching remedy for both the symptoms of their childhood diseases and their adult diseases, it will be dramatically curative. Symptoms from any part of the body or state of mind will be equally useful in the matching process. All symptomatic expressions of the patient (physical, mental and emotional) will be found to represent efforts to heal.

Homeopathy is a holistic form of medicine only because it treats the underlying cause of a disease. Both the process of evaluating the patient's symptoms and making a treatment recommendation needs to include all of the patient's symptoms. The remedy chosen will need to match all of the symptoms. Your treatment will then be in concert with the self-healing intentions of the symptoms. You will then know all of your symptoms to be produced for the express purpose of healing.

Treating patients for the underlying cause of their disease is an entirely different experience than treating the level of secondary symptoms. Your body produces symptoms as a response to an underlying cause. The symptoms represent a secondary reaction to a problem and not a primary condition. It is most important to define symptoms as your healing efforts and they are to be reinforced and not suppressed.

In homeopathic medicine, all symptoms that make up a person's unique experience of life are helpful in finding the best match. No symptom is unrelated to the current or chief complaints. Things that western medicine would consider to be unrelated and not useful in making a diagnosis or treatment recommendation will be important in a form of holistic medicine. There is no part of you or any function of your body that is disconnected from the whole. Every part of you is working together to achieve the best health that is possible for you.

Similarly, in traditional Chinese medicine the meridian lines are understood to energetically interconnect all parts of your body. The meridian system functions as our energy information system. It links all functions and parts of the body together. This system works with a speed and complexity that is orders of magnitude greater than your more stable system of homeostasis that we recognize in western medicine.

The circulation in the blood of factors controlling organ function is important for maintaining stability in your health. The factors controlling health in the blood provide stability and the energetic system provides capability to respond to all influences on your health. Your energetic information system has the complexity to consider all factors that would go into determining your state of health at any moment.

The energetic system is closer to the level where the cause of your symptoms exerts its influence. The energetic system has the ability to detect and respond to all influences that are being imposed upon you to move your health away from the ideal. The "cause" of your symptom complex or disease results from a summation of all these influences. These unbalancing influences can come at the physical, mental or emotional level.

All of your tissues and body functions necessarily have to respond to any challenge you encounter. This response will occur according to the nature of the challenge and the nature of the tissue or function. For example, your knee, stomach and mind are interconnected along the energy meridian known as the stomach meridian. A function of the stomach meridian is to monitor and respond to health challenges that come to its specific locations in the body or particular types of stresses. When you are challenged in any of these ways, you will respond holistically. Your knee can only respond as a knee, though. Your stomach can only respond as a stomach because that is its nature and your mind can only respond as a mind will. All three of these responses will serve the same purpose of maintaining the optimal balance of your health in response to a particular type of challenge.

In Chinese or homeopathic medicine the symptoms of each area of the body or each function of the body will be equally useful in finding the similar energy to augment your response to this challenge. That matching energy will assist you in overcoming this challenge and rebalancing your health in a way that strengthens you. Healing with similar energy will enhance your ability to recognize and respond to this type of challenge in the future.

This holistic appreciation of health will help you understand why the homeopathic physician finds it helpful in treating a condition like rheumatoid arthritis to know if you are thirsty, impatient or warm blooded by nature. The remedy selected will be different for the thirsty, impatient and warm-blooded individual with rheumatoid arthritis than the one selected for the unthirsty, patient and chilly individual. All of these symptoms are related to your response to the underlying cause of your disease. Every symptom you produce, as part of your symptomatic experience of life, is understood in the energetic systems of medicine to have the same purpose—healing. This is known to be the case through the everyday experience of applying the Law of Similars. All physical, emotional and mental symptoms will be equally useful in finding the closest match to work with the body holistically in recovering health.

Observing healing under homeopathic care reaffirms the reality that healing in the human being occurs holistically. All of your symptoms will simultaneously change in the direction of normal when the best possible remedy is found. This process of holistic healing occurs without the doctor or patient needing to direct each detail. Healing is also independent of their intentions or desires.

It may be helpful to define what I mean by everything moving in the "normal" direction with healing. "Normal" means a balanced state that allows you the freedom to respond effectively to a wide variety of stresses. Under energetic treatment, healing moves towards normal in a parallel fashion on the mental, emotional and physical levels. You may notice the physical changes most easily but the mental and emotional changes are occurring simultaneously.

The holistic nature of the evaluation of a patient results in one of the detrimental aspects of homeopathic medicine. Every patient has to be considered as a unique case. The average intake in our office for chronic disease will take from two to three hours. It is possible to move much faster in an acute condition, but in chronic cases taking short cuts will lower your chance of finding the ideal match for the patient.

This lengthy time requirement is a major drawback in homeopathic medicine that puts it out of step with the fast paced expectations of modern medicine. In western medicine we can achieve speed and efficiency by lumping patients together into diagnostic categories. The treatment will then be according to the standard of care for this disease and individualization is not considered appropriate. Medical legal concerns push doctors in the direction of standardization of care and away from individualization.

It is interesting to note that the system of medicine based on the Law of Similars has been unchanged for centuries. Homeopathic medicine has not needed any revisions to its fundamental principles as further details of health and physiology have been discovered. The symptoms that a remedy can cause and cure today are the same as centuries ago. Actual homeopathic remedies are in existence today from nearly 200 years ago that can still be used with the same curative effects that they had when they were manufactured.

The material and energetic properties of substances are apparently stable over time. This reliability indicates that the underlying principle of the Law of Similars is closely aligned with the reality of what determines the balance between health and disease. In modern medicine we often seem to change our minds quickly and easily when it comes to the type of treatment we recommend. It is easy to find groups that argue for very different types of treatment for the same condition. These contradictions make it harder to have confidence that these systems of medicine are really treating the underlying cause of the patient's condition. Modern therapies are more likely to be treating the disease as recognized by its physical manifestation or secondary symptoms than the underlying cause.

It is also worthwhile to examine whether the concepts of all healing as self-healing and like cures like are consistent and compatible. This subject will be the emphasis of the next chapter, so I will only comment that, in my opinion, they are completely compatible. You can make your own determination as other information is added to your perspective on this question.

It is possible to draw some conclusions from combining the information presented in chapters two and three. You want to combine the concepts of all healing is self-healing and like cures like. Studying these concepts together gives us a theoretical basis for understanding the meaning of symptoms and the process of healing. Practicing homeopathic medicine, for the physician, and taking homeopathic remedies, for the patient, brings thee theoretical concepts of energetic healing from an abstract concept into a state of concrete reality.

I did not have a grasp of these concepts when I was practicing traditional orthopedic surgery. Though it was not an intention of mine initially in learning alternative medicine, the practice of adding complementary medicine to my practice has made these concepts undeniable. Observing energetic healing makes the practice of medicine more beneficial to the patient and the practitioner.

It is harder for a medically trained person to open their mind to this understanding than how easily patients seem to accept these concepts. After observing the results of energetic healing, it is my firm conclusion that the potential to heal any and all conditions is an inherent capability of the human being (with the exception of a complete absence of the tissue to be healed by some congenital or traumatic reason). A need to heal and the capability to heal is something that stays with you your whole life.

Several years ago one of my orthopedic patients helped me learn that a person's state of health has continuity over their whole life. Stuart was a World War II veteran who needed surgery for painfully worn out shoulders. Surgery had been successful a few years before in mostly relieving the pain in one of his shoulders and giving him back useful motion and strength. When he came back to get his other shoulder fixed the cardiologist and anesthesiologist would not clear him for surgery. Stuart was complaining of chest pains, shortness of breath, great fatigue and exhausting sweats and chills at night making it hard for him to get any rest.

Stuart turned out to be quite an interesting case once you spent more time going over his history. He wasn't just another case of rotator cuff tendonitis and degeneration of the shoulder. He had served in the South Pacific during the war and received the standard issue prophylaxis for malaria. He had contracted a mild case, as had many other soldiers, and recovered without any subsequent problems.

Something had apparently changed in Stuart's health over time to lower his resistance to disease and the heart disease he was being treated for now in some way bore a relationship to his state of health fifty years ago. I gave him the homeopathic remedy indicated for his old and new symptoms together. It was the most common remedy used in homeopathy to treat malaria. His health improved dramatically and the symptoms of his heart disease diminished along with the fevers and sweats.

As you progress through the chapters of this book, keep the intention in your mind to *relate* similar observations and experiences with *the process of healing to your understanding of the meaning of symptoms and diseases.* As your understanding progresses, you will be better equipped to remove any present obstacles to your enjoyment of life as well as prevent future health problems.

I have often instructed people in using the homeopathic method of healing to treat themselves for a burn. The homeopathic treatment of burns will offer you a nice example of the power of the Law of Similars and the self-healing process. Quite a few people have tried this treatment and reported their stories back and how amazed they were when they tried it. The pain, redness and swelling that they expected to have from their burn was greatly reduced by the homeopathic approach to treatment. The homeopathic treatment is very simple and requires no pharmacy or special equipment.

The homeopathic treatment of burns is appropriate for first and second degree burns. Deeper second degree burns or third degree burns also have equally effective treatments but they require the use of specific remedies to control the pain of the burn and speed the healing and prevent secondary infection. For more serious burns you should consult a homeopathic physician or guidelines published in homeopathic medical texts.

If you experience a burn on part of your body, the homeopathic treatment would be to bring the part of the body that has been burned back into the proximity of a source of heat. You need only to bring the burned part close enough to the source of heat to experience a tolerable amount of discomfort for an instant (a second or two). Then withdraw the burned part away from the source of heat. You are treating like with like—a burn to the body with heat. Be moderate in your therapeutic exposure to the source of heat—not enough to cause injury but also not too little to have a healing effect. If you are sensitive, you can repeat a more mild exposure to the heat a few times until the pain is relieved.

You will normally experience a strikingly different healing response to the original burn. The amount of pain, swelling and redness will be much less than expected. The total healing time will be much shorter also. Once you have this experience, your mind will be opened to the reality that you have an alternative system of healing. You might wonder, as I did, how are we able to heal so comfortably and without the usual inflammatory process that I expected. The burned part will heal and be just as normal as any previous experiences you have had with burns. I admit that it takes a little courage and faith to try this the first time, but you will find it very worth your while.

It may be helpful to draw a contrast between homeopathic treatment and allopathic medicine in this simple example. You may be familiar with putting ice or cold on a burn. This is the western principle of treating **against** the cause of the symptoms. The ice may be equally effective in reducing the pain initially but you eventually will experience the inflammation of the healing process as redness, swelling and pain. When the ice is removed the pain may quickly return and even feel worse. It may require longer or more constant applications of the ice to bring relief. After a time the cold may not even be very helpful.

There will be a distinct difference using the principle of treating like with like. One brief treatment can be sufficient to entirely control the healing response. This simple example presents a powerful and curious experience of your potential for healing utilizing the Law of Similars and self-healing. The results, the efficiency and the cost are remarkably different.

The Law of Similars is the process that has been given to you, in our world, to efficiently recover the best health that you can have according to your individual potential. As you continue to explore further concepts and examples of healing, it becomes obvious that symptoms and healing are a basic purpose and process of life. This statement is beyond the level of proof presented so far. Keep these ideas in mind as you attempt to prove or disprove it to yourself. Base your judgment on your past experiences and the application of these new concepts to the future occurrences in your life.

At the least, I would like to recommend that being optimistic about your healing potential is quite reasonable. It appears that our world contains the mechanism and the materials that can be used reliably to remove symptoms or heal from diseases. The world will indeed provide challenges, stresses and accidents that interrupt your enjoyment of life. There is also the mechanism provided for you to recover from these adverse situations. It does not seem logical that this would be all random or accidental. There must be logic to the state of reality you are experiencing. As you continue to build up experiences with the rules and process of healing, hopefully the logic of the process can be seen. Gaining awareness of the logic can increase the efficiency of your response to the challenges of your life. Hopefully, greater comfort and ease will replace dis-ease.

Your Healing Heart

AWARENESS

All Healing is Self-Healing

Law of Similars =
The Healing Law of Nature

Healing = Transforming
Susceptibility into Resistance

Vital Force = "The Big You"

The Disease of Fear

ACCEPTANCE

Changing Your Perception of Reality

Being Open-Minded to
Alternative Views of Reality

**It's OK to Talk to Yourself
and Listen to Your Body**

The Amazing Human Being

Western Medicine has Value
as a Healing System

FORGIVENESS

The Meaning of Symptoms and Disease

You're OK

Healing: The Never Ending Story
= Learning and Healing Through
Life's Opportunities and Challenges

Chapter 4

It's OK to Talk to Yourself—The Meaning of Symptoms

It takes a combination of both open-mindedness and courage to change your existing perception of who you are and ask what factors are contributing to you being the person that you are. This chapter helps you examine the evidence indicating that the answer to this question will be closer to the truth when approached holistically. Your physical health has the same purpose and the same cause as does your state of mental and emotional health.

You are being instructed to search for the meaning and the cause of your state of health in order to find an effective way of improving your health. It is reasonable to ask why or from where might you get the inclination or courage to examine this question? The motivation may come from a disease or some limitation on your ability to enjoy life. It may also come from a desire or intuition telling you that more is available to you than you are now able to experience or understand. Whatever might be your motivation, the time and effort you put into searching for the meaning behind your state of health can greatly benefit you now and in the future.

It may be helpful to start with the perspective taught in American medical schools and then draw a comparison with holistic medicine. This more familiar understanding of symptoms as the problem can serve as your baseline of comparison with a more holistic understanding of the meaning of symptoms. How you perceive the meaning of your own symptoms may be strongly influenced by the cultural and social situations that surround you. It will tend to reinforce your opinions, if that same perspective is present in the medical profession.

Keep in mind that the western view of symptoms is just one perspective. Exposing yourself to alternative views of the meaning of a symptom adds another perspective. This process of expanding your perspective of the purpose of symptoms should not be feared and may be beneficial in understanding the cause of your state of health. Having alternative perspectives available to you adds the complexity of choice in selecting a treatment, but opens up other possible resources that may be beneficial to your health.

The meaning of symptoms in western medicine is clear. They are seen as the problem. Patients see their symptoms as the problem. They take their symptoms to the doctor to have them removed and the problem solved. The doctor's impression is usually the same. The symptoms are the problem that has brought this patient in for treatment and it is the doctor's job to get rid of this problem symptom. If symptoms are seen as the problem, it would only be logical to work against the body process that is producing the symptoms.

It is important to recognize the western perspective on the meaning of symptoms. It helps you understand the logic that results in an attack being made on the body and its symptoms. It is a common state of mind in western medicine that the physicians are "attacking" the disease state. It would only be logical for you to allow this attack or participate in an attack on your body, if you understand some body part or function as being viewed in error or as the problem. The western view of a symptom or a diseased part of the body is that it needs to be removed (surgically or with radiation and drugs) because it represents the problem.

Appendicitis is a fairly common condition that can illustrate the view of western medicine towards an illness. A patient with the symptoms of the disease appendicitis is clearly sick. His abdominal pain, nausea and fever represent a complex of problems. The diagnosis is based upon this collection of symptoms. The diagnosis and the cause of his problem will be understood to be appendicitis. No further depth of understanding of the cause of his symptoms need be considered to determine the treatment. The treatment is clear once the diagnosis is established—surgery—a clear attack on the body—with a good likelihood of a prompt correction of the "problem" and "full" recovery. Hold this example in your mind as we consider if the recovery actually is complete and if the real problem has been dealt with.

The approach that is taken in energetic, holistic medicine is quite different from this western type of attack on the symptoms and the body. This difference results from an almost opposite appreciation for the meaning and purpose of symptoms. The differences can be summed up as between one that works against the body ("anti") or with the body (similars).

Two centuries of homeopathic literature and experience contain numerous examples of patients with the symptoms of appendicitis being successfully treated with homeopathic remedies. These remedies are ones that are known to be able to produce symptoms very similar to the condition we know as appendicitis. In most cases, no surgery would be required and full recovery achieved, even in cases of ruptured appendix and abscess. This experience was gained primarily in the nineteenth century when surgery was much more dangerous than it is today.

In 1998 Wadsworth, Ohio had a rash of cases coming to the hospital emergency room that looked like appendicitis. The symptoms were especially common in students of high school age and within a week the "epidemic" began to escalate. A few early cases went to surgery and had their appendix removed. Quite a few people were admitted to the hospital to be observed for appendicitis.

One of the operating room nurse's sons came down with the symptoms of possible appendicitis and she relayed his symptoms while we were working on an orthopedic case. Based on his symptoms, it was decided to give him a homeopathic remedy during his initial observation period in the hospital. He responded promptly with relief of all his complaints. Since these cases of "possible appendicitis" were presumably based on some sort of communicable process, we were then able to give the same remedy to anyone with the same symptoms and most of them promptly got well and avoided any surgery or hospitalization. These results are not research, just the practice of medicine. It will never be known what exactly was the cause of this situation but the patients were helped in their recovery.

Symptoms still convey the same meaning and importance whether you have an isolated case of disease or a group of people with the same symptoms. When you look at differences in treating symptoms of other common diseases, it can help highlight the different approaches to the treatment of symptoms in pharmaceutical medicine and holistic medicine.

"Anti"histamines are common forms of treatment for the symptoms of hay fever in western medicine. In an allergic reaction, the body produces large amounts of histamine as part of its exaggerated response to pollen. The immune system recognizes the pollen as a harmful substance and creates the elevated level of histamine as part of its defense.

It is an effective treatment for hay fever to pharmaceutically block the body's ability to produce an immune response with drugs such as antihistamines. Because the drugs have an effect on all the tissues of the body, you will tend to experience some side effects from their use in addition to the helpful effects of reducing symptoms of hay fever. Antihistamines are clearly able to relieve symptoms and decrease suffering associated with hay fever. The deeper question for you will be, is there any healing occurring with this anti form of treatment? You can see from our example in chapter three of the treatment of hay fever with the onion that homeopathy presents a very different approach than that of western medicine.

In our hay fever example, it can be clearly seen that treatment with antihistamines is symptomatic only. The symptoms we are familiar with as hay fever are a secondary effect of some underlying cause. The underlying cause of hay fever is not usually considered or investigated in western medicine. Hay fever symptoms represent an immune system that is not functioning in a optimal manner. Their cause will be reconsidered holistically in chapter ten.

In hay fever, we recognize normal parts of the environment as harmful, when these substances do not inherently have an toxic or dangerous effect on human tissues. It is often the case, that for some years before the development of hay fever, the same substances in our environment were contacted and recognized as safe. They previously did not cause an allergic response by the immune system. The allergic reaction is a defensive antigen-antibody reaction by the immune system, whose function is to protect the body from all harmful influences.

There has been some event occur that initiates an altered antibody antigen response to pollen. This event will be the ultimate cause of the hay fever. The symptoms of hay fever are an expression of our body's reaction to this underlying cause and the symptoms should not be misconstrued as the real cause of the problem. **This is a very important distinction!** The results of treatment will depend upon whether you are treating the underlying cause or the secondary symptoms. A curative treatment that deals with the cause of the symptoms may return the immune system to its prior healthy state.

The results of any treatment have to be looked at in a longer time frame to be able to tell if they are having an effect at the secondary level of symptoms or the more primary level of the cause of the condition. The immediate results may be the same for different types of treatment—the relief of suffering. The comfort associated with recovery may stop us from looking any deeper, as the problem will appear to have been solved.

In order to know the level of action of the treatment, it is necessary to take the longer-term consequences of a treatment into consideration. Important long-term results that indicate the level of action of the treatment (cause or symptom) are several and include:

1. The appearance of side effects
2. The recurrence of the symptoms upon discontinuing treatment
3. The return of previous symptoms

An overall improvement in signs of good health. Each of these four long term results will help you know the level at which the treatment you have chosen is affecting your health. This evaluation will let you know if the type of treatment you have chosen is working at the level of cause or secondary symptoms.

Different methods of treatment can give good results in controlling your symptoms and relieving suffering. The question is what type of healing is occurring. Is this a treatment that is strengthening you, or not?

A treatment that is directed at the reason the body is producing symptoms will clearly strengthen the patient's overall health. This statement is based upon the recognition that we each have a "vital force" that is directing our health in response to the events occurring in our life. Your vital force is always acting in a way that is best for your overall health.

Your vital force is not limited like the conscious mind is in its awareness or understanding of the influences on your health. The concept of your vital force will be addressed more thoroughly in the next chapter. Just assume, for now, that this is the case as you interpret what the long-term results of various types of treatment can tell you about the level of action of your treatment choices.

Treatments that are directed at the cause of your symptoms will tend to *not* produce side effects. Treatments that only deal with symptoms will tend to cause side effects. This is an important difference for your understanding in making choices among possible treatments. This difference is logical and to be expected if symptoms are understood to be the purposeful actions of your body to heal itself.

If the healing actions of your body (symptoms) are overpowered with a drug or surgery, and the underlying cause is not dealt with, your body will still recognize a need for corrective action. In this situation, the body will produce new symptoms in its attempt to recover health. Western medicine calls these actions of your body side effects because they were not the intention of the original prescribed treatment. I would have to say this is an ingenious use of language to obscure real effects of the prescribed treatment.

A changing picture of symptoms will be viewed differently from a holistic perspective of healing. The appearance of new symptoms (as side effects) without a new cause of disease would not be expected. In the case of side effects the drugs become the new cause of disease. In a holistic medicine where the "vital force" is presumed to be directing the production of symptoms as part of the recovery response, it would not be logical for your body to move the healing response to other outlets of expression.

All symptoms are healing attempts of the body. This includes what we call side effects. The original symptoms were the body's most efficient path of recovery. Side effects represent less efficient means that have become necessary due to the prescribed treatment working against the actions of your vital force.

This is not going to be an easy pill for the drug industry to swallow, but notice that you can't find a drug that does not have known side effects. In contrast, energetic therapies are not known to have any side effects. I cannot overemphasize the importance of letting this difference become part of your process of evaluating treatment choices and your understanding of your natural healing capabilities. This huge difference comes directly from the level at which the various treatments work: one at the level of cause and one at the level of secondary effects (symptoms).

The likelihood of your symptoms returning after the treatment has been discontinued will also help you to know if a treatment has been curative or symptomatic. The long-term results from various treatments again will be strikingly different. You need only step back and observe the long-term changes in your health or lack of changes in your health to clearly see distinct differences demonstrating if the treatment is against or with the vital force. Your insight into the meaning and purpose of symptoms will be increased by observing the long-term results of your various treatmentoptions looked at from the perspective of these four criterion.

A purely symptomatic treatment may be able to completely remove the present symptoms, but it is not likely going to prevent recurrences of the same problem in the future. This is commonly seen in children with recurrent ear infections. A course of antibiotics and drainage, if needed, will help the child recover his health, and feel fine for a time, but the ear infection can return again in just as bad a form as it was originally. The treatment can be repeated again with success but does not lessen the likelihood of another infection occurring or lessen its severity or increase the time interval before the infection returns. The ear infection may evolve into a more resistant variety with repeated doses of an anti-biotic treatment.

The long-term results of energetic, holistic therapy will present a very different picture. Children with recurrent ear infections begun on homeopathic treatment will also recover their health when the correct matching remedy is found. It is still possible that he or she will get further ear infections, but there will be a noticeable change. Each subsequent ear infection will be less severe than prior ones, and if treated with the matching remedy, they will start to occur less often. The ear infections should either completely stop, or become quite infrequent, as treatment is repeated. These are historical findings from two centuries of experience and new, long-term studies need to be done to document the results. These experiences need to be brought from the anecdotal level to the level of statistical significance gained from large studies, done over a longer period of time.

Another interesting observation seen in homeopathic medicine is the phenomenon of recurrence of old symptoms. This phenomenon gives you some insight into the different sites of action of your treatment options. Return of previous symptoms seems to occur routinely only in an energetic treatment such as homeopathy. This phenomenon is not seen in treatments that can be presumed to be only symptomatic and that have only short-term effects. This phenomenon of return of old symptoms can give you an insight into your healing capabilities that is almost the direct opposite to the occurrence of side effects under treatment.

I never encountered this phenomenon of return of old symptoms when I only practiced surgery and drug based medicine. I now see this phenomenon fairly commonly when the homeopathic remedy selected for a patient is a very close match to all of their symptoms. Symptoms that the patient has had at a previous time in their life will often reappear early in homeopathic treatment when the potency selected and its frequency of repetition is higher than what would be ideal.

The situation of using an overly strong potency of a homeopathic remedy creates a rush of healing where symptoms from previous times in the patient's life will reappear. It is likely that the remedy given would also have been indicated for the previous symptoms when they originally occurred. Recurrence of old symptoms is commonly seen when the treatment originally given for the symptoms was symptomatic or with an "anti" type of approach. The symptoms that reappear will be recognizable as a condition having occurred previously in the patient's life but will reappear with considerably less severity. They will often last a short period of time and leave spontaneously or when the dosage is reduced. If the condition should reappear a second or third time it will be milder each time and last a shorter time. Several recurrences are often the case, if the previous condition was a fairly chronic condition in the past or recurred many times.

The phenomenon of recurrence of previous symptoms under homeopathic treatment indicates that the patient is beginning a process that will lead to a quite remarkable recovery of their health. Unfortunately, it is not possible to know or test the mechanism at work here with any certainty. My impression is that the tissues of the body maintain a memory (? immunologic) of past events that are subject to treatment or recurrence at any time.

Under the influence of a deeply curative therapy, you are able to chronologically wind your health backwards and revisit conditions in a way that can complete healing that was only partially completed initially. This is speculative, of course, and requires a much longer-term perspective and better statistical data than just my conjecture or deductive reasoning.

The fourth area for your consideration of the different long-term effects of symptomatic or curative treatments is also an area that is difficult to be objective. The goal is to observe the varying results of treatment in being able to produce an improvement in the overall signs of good health.

The practice of orthopedic surgery did not offer a good perspective to observe this in any long term way. I cannot discount that this may occur with surgery and drug therapy. In much of western medicine, the specialist take a very focused appraisal of the patient and does not step back and make a long term assessment of the impact of our treatment on all the mental, emotional and physical aspects of the person's life. I clearly saw some surgeries as a pivotal event in people's lives. Surgery may help people recover their mobility or comfort. That can translate into a major turnaround in their life.

Practicing holistic medicine does give a clear impression that when the underlying cause of the patient's symptoms is identified and treated, they will generally make a recovery that includes all spheres of their life. In a holistic recovery, you will experience a wide range of beneficial effects beyond removal of the symptoms. This can include having more energy, sleeping better, more mental clarity, physical comfort and a sense of emotional equanimity or balance in your life.

In homeopathy, you can see the recovery of these parameters of health follow a cause and effect relationship with the repetition of the remedy and its potency. With time you will be able to recognize the need for, and the actions of the remedy, as you feel your holistic response to the remedy. When you recognize this, you will have control over your recovery and know when the remedy is needed. This type of therapy may lead to such profound healing that after a time you can maintain your own health and not even need the remedy. The desired end point of treatment would be that you no longer need the remedy or have symptoms that require you to visit your doctor.

The main purpose of this chapter is to introduce the concept that **all of your symptoms are good things.** This concept is based on the principles that have been presented so far. It combines the concept of all healing as self-healing and the Law of Similars. Next, you need to study the evidence that shows the relationship between healing and symptoms.

The reality of experience in energetic healing is that when you give a patient more of the exact energy of their symptoms, they will recover improved health. They will heal and not suffer more. You can also observe that the process of healing, which follows the principle of like curing like, will also demonstrates the nature of true healing as seen through its curative effects. These manifestations of a true cure are the absence of side effects, improved resistance to diseases, healing of previous conditions and an overall increase in signs of good health. These results make it difficult to deny that the process of working with your symptoms can achieve many positive results and few negative ones.

It is useful to observe that it is necessary to match the entire symptomatic experience of the patient's life in choosing the remedy that has the potential to be most curative. It is necessary to give you the very same energy of your symptoms to stimulate the process of you healing yourself. This fact indicates that *no symptom is without usefulness for your healing.* Your experience in the world takes on a very different meaning, when all of those things you may see as your sufferings, take on usefulness for healing. Your symptoms can be interpreted as your mechanism to overcome a particular challenge in life. I will discuss later how it may be that your challenges in life represent your potential opportunities for growth.

The observation that healing occurs holistically also reinforces the concept that *your body simultaneously produces a specific set of symptoms to overcome each challenge.* As recovery occurs under homeopathic treatment, all of your symptoms will recover at the same time. *Under the influence of a well-matched remedy, you will recover simultaneously your physical, mental and emotional health.*

Observing this holistic healing process take place under the influence of energetic remedies makes it appear most convincing that healing is the intention of your symptoms and symptoms are the mechanism of your healing. It is an error to see symptoms only as your sufferings. They represent your opportunity for strengthening and growth in this lifetime. It is, therefore, prudent for you to study the workings of this innate healing mechanism that you have been given. This knowledge will enable you to make the healing process as complete and powerful as possible.

Seeing healing as the purpose of symptoms can be a source of optimism and peace of mind. The book "Spontaneous Remission" demonstrates the possibilities and shows it is reasonable to be optimistic about your chances of recovery, even from very serious diseases. It makes sense to study successful cases in trying to make the process of healing more certain.

Advancing your understanding of the role symptoms play in healing will point you in the right direction. Your optimism can also be enhanced each time you experience healing according to the law of nature (like cures like). Simply treating a burn with heat can open up your mind to a reality you may never want to ignore again. For more serious or chronic diseases, the lack of side effects from treatment and actually recovering signs of good health can produce a result that can be quite amazing.

Knowledge of the capabilities of holistic healing can give you a sense of control over your healing process. A large number of the healing substances of our world have already had their specific healing properties defined. You just need to seek out and find the one that matches your symptoms. Just knowing that the possibility of healing always exists and that you are never suffering needlessly can bring some measure of peace of mind.

You will probably never be completely free of challenges in all aspects of your life, but if they are understood as a process of growth and evolution, they will be less overwhelming. No system of therapy that I have learned is ever 100% effective. Living with imperfections in the ability to understand all the underlying principles of healing and the meaning of your symptoms is an inevitable part of life.

Energetic medicine has also been unable to cure some patients in my hands, but I have not seen it cause side effects or needless suffering. A partial recovery or comfort care may be all that is possible in some cases. Cases that fail to recover usually indicate either the patient or doctor have an incomplete knowledge of all the underlying factors that may be contributing to the disease. Even in the face of failure, it can afford some peace of mind to know that a higher purpose is always being served. It is just beyond our conscious ability to be aware of what that is.

The benefits of becoming aware of the meaning of your symptoms and accepting that the symptoms represent a useful part of the natural healing process can together be empowering. When you reach some level of awareness of the reasons for your symptoms, it is often the first major step in healing. Understanding that *you really are OK, no matter what symptom you are experiencing* can ease suffering and speed healing. You will make overall improvements in your health when your energy shifts from suffering to healing.

It is comforting to be aware that the right symptoms are being produced at all times. Symptoms show you the correct steps to heal and lead you to the right remedy. In homeopathy, you can study the known causes associated with the matching remedy for your symptoms and gain insight into the cause of your symptoms. This awareness helps to relieve the oppression or depression of feeling like a victim of some external influence. Yes, life is challenging you but you are not being defeated by life, you are responding. There is a cause of your problem, but it represents your growth process of overcoming a challenge and potentially be strengthened at the end of the process.

Your symptoms represent your healing reaction to overcome the effects of some challenge that has negatively influenced your health. Working with yourself, by giving yourself more of the same energy as the symptoms you are producing, can bring about your healing gently and quickly. You are responding to a challenge. It is encouraging to know that when you maximize the efforts of your healing symptoms, you can overcome the challenge and recover your health and be strengthened.

Illness may seem less overwhelming if you accept the fact that there is a cause underlying your disease and a process to deal with the cause. You do not just have to control the symptoms. You can use the information from the symptoms to speed healing. This awareness can keep hope alive, that no matter how long a tunnel you may be staring into; there is a light at the end of the tunnel that can be your recovery.

Before leaving this chapter on the meaning of symptoms, I would like to relate a few experiences from studying various alternative systems of medicine over the years. They can shed some interesting light on the healing powers you have available and the healing mechanism. It is not necessary for everyone to study or experience all these different approaches to healing, but it can help you understand the principles that are common among them. These examples of healing may help further deepen your understanding of the meaning of your symptoms.

These examples should help you to be thoroughly impressed by yourself. They all relate to this completely amazing creation that you experience as a human being. You have astounding capabilities to respond to this world in a way that protects and strengthens your state of health.

When I was learning to do acupuncture, a fellow student who treated primarily children, related to me that he had found hypnosis to be very helpful in his acupuncture practice. Patients can be quite apprehensive at first with the thought of being punctured by a number of needles. Some patients faint and others become quite tense and exaggerate their discomfort from the procedure. The American Society of Clinical Hypnosis offers excellent course in hypnosis for professionals, so I decided to take a few courses and see what usefulness this might have in my practice.

I did not find hardly any need for hypnosis in my acupuncture patients but learned something interesting about the human mind. All hypnosis turns out to be self-hypnosis. The hypnotist does facilitate the patient going into a self-hypnotized state, but the patient is completely in control of his actions while hypnotized. Most everyone is completely capable of the amazing acts you see performed while "under" hypnosis.

When you are not under hypnosis, but under the normal control of your conscious mind, you are likely to doubt that you could perform these feats and due to this state of mind you probably could not perform them. When you have allowed yourself to be put under the control of this extra-conscious, hypnotized state, you are then capable of responding to a set of suggestions in a very different way. It is interesting to note the strikingly different capability you can have to respond when under the control of this hypnotized state as compared to your normal conscious or awake state. Your ability to perform these amazing feats somewhat blurs the definition of what is the more awakened state of mind.

The pertinent point to be learned from the hypnotic state is that the symptoms you manifest in response to a stimulus—like being punctured with a needle—can be variable. Your response to a challenge can change according to the perspective you are using to view the event from.

Apparently, the cause and effect relationship between a stress and its secondary symptoms has the potential to be variable. This potential for variability in responding to the events in your life adds another dimension to understanding the meaning of your symptoms. The same inciting cause may result in a different set of symptoms, based upon a different set of surrounding circumstances being present at the time the event occurs.

The significance of this potential for variability that exists in your response to life's events is that reproducible patterns can be discovered, but they will not have absolute predictability. Your symptomatic response (or change in health) is determined by the interplay of vast amounts of information that makes up the holistic experience of life.

It is difficult to be consciously aware of *all* of the past and present influences on your life being utilized to determine your symptomatic response. It is equally difficult to consciously know *all* of your natural strengths and weaknesses that predispose you to a certain type of symptomatic response. Learning your reaction patterns is helpful but you need to remain open-minded to the existence of other perspectives and the potential for change from a past pattern.

I gave up using hypnosis in my practice after a few years, as it was difficult to control the hypnotic effects. It turned out that patients and their families following an injury are very susceptible to hypnosis. I could save myself a lot of time and save the patient an anesthetic by using it in the emergency room to set fractures or reduce dislocations. Hypnosis is a good alternative when the patient had a full stomach or some other problem that the anesthesiologist wanted to wait 6 to 8 hours for the stomach to clear before general anesthesia was safe.

Following an injury, patients easily reach a deep level of hypnosis where they are not aware of the pain as the fracture is set. The only difficulty was that often the patient's relatives and the emergency room nurse could also become hypnotized.

The first time this happened to me was disconcerting. I was called down to the ER to see a high school football player with a dislocated elbow. He was still in his full uniform due to the painful and unstable arm. His stomach was full of snacks and pop, so anesthesia wanted to wait six hours for the stomach to clear, which would have been almost midnight.

The patient was quite uncomfortable and the arm needed to be fixed. Giving him narcotics for pain would slow down the emptying of the stomach and delay the process even further. The family and I both wanted to just get it fixed and not have to wait till late at night, so I offered him a try at hypnosis to reduce the elbow. He was agreeable and so I hypnotized him easily and reduced the elbow dislocation with minimal effort as he was quite relaxed.

Once the arm had been reduced, I realized I didn't have anyone left to help me hold his arm while the splint was applied. His mom and the ER nurse were both in a hypnotic trance. It was going to hard to bring the nurse back without bringing the patient out of their hypnotic state prior to getting the splint on. This situation always amazed me as E.R. nurses are about as thick-skinned people as you might come by, due to the constant barrage of calamities they witness.

It was actually at the sincere urging of a complete stranger that my "terminally curious" state was again stimulated to study a new area, craniosacral therapy. Craniosacral therapy can help you at times better understand a hidden meaning your symptoms may represent. Learning craniosacral therapy included studying the process of somato-emotional release (SER). This form of therapy has been investigated and refined by Dr. John Upledger.

The state of awareness available during SER adds another interesting perspective to your investigation of the meaning of symptoms. The SER process goes way beyond hypnosis in that it allows you to communicate with your patient simultaneously on both the conscious and the extra-conscious level.

In the SER process, the patient is also in control of the therapy. The therapist uses the techniques of SER to bring the extra-conscious level of his patient's awareness into communication with the patient's conscious mind. The therapist can then ask questions of the extra-conscious awareness. The question you especially want an answer to is: what is the reason the patient is producing the specific symptoms that are a limiting complaint in their life. This is an extremely powerful technique. SER is not to be taken lightly and requires both a gifted and experienced therapist to be helpful. The level of insight that can be achieved is powerful enough to relieve the patient of the current consequences from stresses occurring at a previous time in their life and not add any new ones.

SER does have the potential to go right to the core level of the cause of your symptoms, and for that reason, I think needs to be explored by medicine in a much wider way. It can be quite valuable in difficult and resistant cases where other attempts to treat the patient have not worked. It may allow you to move past a resistance or blockage to your achieving awareness that then permits you to understand and resolve the underlying cause of your problem. Often, you may get stuck in a reaction pattern that need to be re-evaluated in the light of a more mature understanding, and then allow its resolution and healing.

It didn't take any time at all for me to experience the power of SER and what it can tell you about hidden complexities in knowing the cause of a patient's symptoms. In my introductory class, we were practicing the technique in groups of four people. All four of the members of my group were fairly experienced therapists. One of the therapists volunteered to be the patient as she had an issue that had remained unresolved despite many attempts at correction. She had always been more overweight than she would have liked and was unable to find the reason that she would chronically over eat.

This seemed like a fair question to ask the body. We set about waiting for her craniosacral rhythm to tell us it was comfortable with us asking her the question. When she was ready, we asked her to go to the time in her life when the reason for her over eating occurred. She consented to do this, and soon related that she had arrived at this time in her life. She could feel it was the correct time, but she was not able to see anything to know where she was or what was happening. With a little more time she was able to hear a voice and she recognized that it was her mother's voice. She was able to relate to us a conversation that was occurring. Her mother was telling her husband that she was pregnant. This was met with a very angry response from the father. He did not want any more children, and especially at that time. She related the feelings she was experiencing at that time and the feelings of her mother.

This SER practice session brought out very strong emotions for our "patient-therapist". She realized that she had accepted blame for this unwanted pregnancy and carried this deep discomfort, as guilt, her entire life. She had developed the compensatory mechanism of taking in excess amounts of comfort food to balance this internally held discomfort. The comfort food was a purposeful self-medication, to balance the internal discomfort she felt.

I can say that I was personally stunned. The skeptic in me is always looming large and this whole scenario seemed impossible based upon my existing concept of human capabilities. How could an unborn child be aware of this and make a "conscious" decision to react and set a pattern of behavior in action, that could persist through to adult life? Is this SER a fanciful dream or could it be real? Though it would require a lot of courage on her part, it seemed inescapable that we would have to have confirmation from her mother to know if this was a true occurrence.

It is certainly true to say that my lab partners and I were anxiously anticipating the next morning. We were about to be either thrown into a new awareness of the reality of our world or realize our gullibility was going to negate any true learning in this course. The report was quite sobering. When our volunteer had called her mother that evening, to relate her experience in class, her mother was as startled as we were. Her mother related that to the best of her recollection, the conversation was a verbatim recounting of the conflict that actually did occur when she five months pregnant with her daughter.

I have never been more astounded to learn of how little we really appreciate of the amazing capabilities of the human being. Still to this day, I can recall the sensation of awe I was hit with, when she relayed that all that we had experienced the day before was an actual occurrence, some forty years before. It should be humbling to realize just how limited we are in our perception of all the reasons that might be contributing factors to the cause of our symptoms. In the acute situation, cause and effect may be easy to know. In the chronic situation, all of your preconceived notions must be looked at with some skepticism.

Fortunately, the rules of treatment that are available to you, like the Law of Similars, maintain their validity in the face of some uncertainty in knowing the cause of your symptoms. These examples of the vast nature of human capability and complexity serve to keep you humble in your estimation of how thoroughly you can understand the specific cause, in any individual, of a chronic symptom.

Having caution in your evaluation of the cause of your symptoms should be balanced by having confidence in knowing the truth of the principles of healing. The complexities of life need not cause despair for either yourself or your therapist. Your body seems to produce all the information that is needed to heal itself. This information comes to you in the manner of symptoms and can be found out by the forms of communication you are now exploring.

These examples help reinforce the need for individualization in dealing with any case of a chronic disease. Lumping people together into convenient diagnostic categories bears no resemblance to the reality of the variety of causes for their condition. A patient's unique expression of their disease must be considered in approaching any meaningful understanding of the purpose that their symptoms are serving for them. Fortunately for the medial profession, people will have similarities in their experiences and personalities, so the number of symptoms is not unlimited and unworkable.

Hypnosis and SER give us some insight into the capabilities you have for compartmentalizing your experiences of life. Some of your memories are carried with you on a conscious level. A much greater amount of information is held in levels of awareness outside of your conscious mind.

I can't offer any help on why certain information remains available to your recall and other information is inaccessible. You can expect that all this information is having an impact on your state of health. It is hard to say how you choose which compartment of the mind to put specific experiences into. This is the case for everyone you ever meet as well as yourself.

Your conscious awareness of both who you are and who they are is but a little part of the whole truth. It is a lot easier to focus on the physical, as this can be more exactly defined than the other aspects that make up the human condition. It is a common blind spot in your evaluation of the world to assume that all others think as you do and react for reasons that would be the same as yours.

The last tool, for this chapter, in learning how to listen to your body and "talk" to yourself will be kinesiology. There are a couple of reasons that might motivate you to develop this skill. First, the more proficient you become in communicating with yourself, the more accurate understanding you will have of who you are and why you are the person that you are. Learning what you "know" beyond the awareness you have in your conscious mind has the potential to help you avoid discomfort and enjoy greater pleasure in life. Last, having a more complete understanding of the complexities involved in each individual's personality and the events that have influenced their life will enhance your compassion for each other. On a larger scale this has the potential to make our world a safer and more enjoyable place.

Kinesiology is a more common diagnostic tool in chiropractic medicine than in western medicine. In western medicine, we have come to rely more and more on laboratory evaluations and less on physical diagnostic skills. Kinesiology is a learned skill of asking questions of the patient and looking for the answers in a muscle response. The patient's conscious mind and voice are not where you look for the answer. The question is directed at the extra-conscious self, who will answer questions in a yes or no format with a predetermined muscle response.

Kinesiology seems a little like a manifestation of one's imagination until you have practiced it a bit. The weak point in the system is mostly in the person asking the questions and not in the accuracy of the answers you will receive. Questions have to be clear and put in a form that can be answered with a yes or no. It is possible to double blind yourself in questioning to ensure that you are getting an answer that is reproducible. Certain systems have developed test vials and similar blank vials to test your accuracy until the answers are the same each time.

It is important to ask the question in an unbiased manner without the intention of producing an expected or desired response. The correct answers will come from the patient. The difficulty is in making sure that the question you are asking is not biased by your personal issues or prejudices. This will detract from receiving accurate information from the patient.

There is the potential with kinesiology for your extra-conscious self to be reacting with the patient's extra-conscious self. This interaction may cause the answers to questions to be misinterpreted. As long as you can put your issues out of the way, you can get directly at the patient's information. This system allows you to ask questions of the patient either verbally or nonverbally and get the same answer. This allows you to bypass the patient's conscious bias, and get to the level of the reasons why they have a particular problem.

Dr. Nambudripad's NAET system is the most impressive of the several kinesiology based systems I have learned. Her system has been developed primarily to treat allergies. She has found that the allergic reaction represents a generalized response of the body to stress. The stress can originate holistically, at the physical, mental or emotional level and often the causative stress is fear or anxiety. She has developed a routine of detecting where the tissue memory of the stress is held in the body and what is the basis for the body's protective reaction against the specific allergen.

The NAET technique allows the body to be reprogrammed where the association between the allergen and the original event that initiated this protective response is broken. Once this has been accomplished, the allergic response does not occur when the previously allergic substance is contacted. Your body will not associate that substance any longer with the stress. The substance will not be recognized as harmful any longer.

The NAET system allows patients to free themselves of allergies. If it is desired, in the process of questioning the patient, the original cause of the allergic response can be sought. Knowing the cause of the allergy can strengthen you in a way that may help prevent the recurrence of a similar response in the future. The tissues of your body hold the history of all this information and it can be found for your benefit. It takes a little practice to get it right but this form of communication (kinesiology) gives you a powerful tool to recovering your health and discovering the meaning of your symptoms. It allows you to profit from the experiences that you are having in your life and not just suffer from them.

The experiences gained from a NAET practice reinforce that you do not suffer needlessly from your allergies. All allergies have a purpose. When this purpose can be recognized and served, you can profit from it. This insight and the experience of seeing it in practice reinforces an optimistic world view that the world provides everything needed to profit from your experience of life. The better choice seems to be to recognize this potential when you look for answers to why you are experiencing "dis-ease".

You need not suffer without the potential for recovery or benefiting from the process of suffering. To find the answer to relieve suffering may require you to explore a wider range of perspectives and possibilities. You often need to look beyond the more obvious physical state and the conscious level of awareness. The extra-conscious dimension and the unique mental-emotional aspects of your personality may contain equally important answers to resolve your sufferings.

For all the reasons presented in this chapter, medicine in the 21st century needs to advance in the area of learning to listen to your body and being comfortable in talking with your own self. You need to learn to be a better observer of the patterns of cause and effect producing your state of health. You can learn new patterns of association and susceptibilities. We have developed, to a very high degree, a physically based system of laboratory evaluations, but have not seen a corresponding increase in our ability to understand the cause of disease, and correct the problems at that level.

Much of our very costly system maintains a level of suffering as a chronic disease state. There often may be no expectation of recovery and no attempt made to seek the underlying cause. Increasing the powers of laboratory medicine to the level of the genetic code will probably not get us any closer to the answer. It is the factors that influence how our genetic potential is expressed at different times in your life that really matters.

You cannot look at the changes that occurred in your DNA and know what the causes of this changed expression were. The breakthrough that is needed is in reoriented your thinking. You need to look more holistically and less microscopically.

The answers appear to be available out there for you. We need to learn how to ask better questions. I am optimistic that a new age of diagnostic medicine is not that far off. The expense of the present system, as well as a critical appraisal of the results it produces, will force a change. So, be patient and optimistic. This represents a radical change for both the medical profession and yourself.

Your Healing Heart

Awareness

All Healing is Self-Healing

Law of Similars =
The Healing Law of Nature

**Healing = Transforming
Susceptibility into Resistance**

Vital Force = "The Big You"

The Disease of Fear

Acceptance

Changing Your Perception of Reality

Being Open-Minded to
Alternative Views of Reality

It's OK to Talk to Yourself
and Listen to Your Body

The Amazing Human Being

Western Medicine has Value
as a Healing System

Forgiveness

The Meaning of Symptoms and Disease

You're OK

Healing: The Never Ending Story
= Learning and Healing Through
Life's Opportunities and Challenges

Chapter 5

Susceptibility and Resistance—Healing as Transformation

Exploring the meaning of susceptibility and resistance will help you gain more insight into the mechanism and purpose of healing. The focus will be on the process of changing a susceptibility into a resistance as part of the transformative process of healing. The healing process and its purpose will become more clearly evident through investigating the experience of moving from a state of health to a state of disease and back again to health. Examining the concept of susceptibility helps to break down this transformative, healing process into its steps. Hopefully, this insight will give you a deeper grasp of what is occurring and why.

Susceptibility and resistance are medical words for states of health that have some parallel to the concepts of a weakness or strength. You will have as a unique individual some degree of either susceptibility or resistance towards every potential stress that can occur in life.

Any substance that you may come into contact with has the potential to cause illness. You will either react to it or not react to it depending upon your susceptibility or resistance to it. The potential number of negative influences that we can contact is very large. In an allergic reaction, you have become susceptible to substances that are not normally recognized as dangerous. No two people are likely to have the same exact combination of potential stresses that they have either a susceptibility to or a resistance towards.

All investigations into what are your susceptibilities need to be individualized to be able to treat you at the level of what is causing you to have symptoms. Therefore, learning what your susceptibilities are becomes an important step in determining your best treatment option.

This process of finding your susceptibilities can help determine the cause of your symptoms and also help you find the most effective treatments. This depth of understanding why you have the health you do may allow your treatments to be both effective in relieving symptoms and preventing recurrences of similar symptoms.

In our discussion of susceptibility, it may be helpful to define a few other concepts that relate to healing. It can be routinely observed that the same inciting cause will create a wide range of reactions in different people. If one member of a family is exposed to the flu, all other members of the family will then be exposed. The type of symptoms each family member develops will be similar, in general, but there will be differences in the severity and duration of the symptoms and also some variation in the type of symptoms each family member demonstrates.

Sensitivity relates to the amount of a particular substance, that an individual needs to come into contact with in order to bring about a reaction. A person's level of sensitivity is also unique to them. Their level of sensitivity will usually be fairly consistent over a wide range of substances. There will be many substances that you do not have a susceptibility to and you will have no reaction when coming into contact with them. For those substances you are susceptible to, you will have a fairly constant level of sensitivity, or threshold amount that will incite a reaction

Another concept that helps define your reactions to things is that of **vitality**. Your vitality relates to the strength or violence of the reaction your body will produce when a susceptibility has been triggered. Much the same as the concept of sensitivity, a person's level of vitality will remain fairly constant in their reactions to various substances at various times in life. Ageing and the cumulative effect of stress may slowly lower your vitality. Efforts you make to strengthen yourself (diet, rest, exercise, etc.) can help to raise your vitality. If you use the same definitions for the terms sensitivity and vitality, it will make it easier for you to follow the discussions about susceptibility and healing.

It is also important to *think holistically in understanding the concept of susceptibility.* Each person has a unique set of mental and emotional susceptibilities as well as their physical susceptibilities. It is easier to recognize when one of your susceptibilities has been triggered on the physical level. You can be quite sure what has happened, for example, when you got caught unprepared in a cold rain and then developed a runny nose and cold.

You will have a similar reaction when one of your susceptibilities has been encountered on the mental and emotional level. The cause and effect relationship may be less apparent to you, when the circumstances originate at the mental-emotional level. This is especially true where the condition is chronic and some time has passed since the original causative event occurred. Often in chronic situations the cause may be an ongoing irritation at a lower intensity level. The level of stress may only subtly parallel the intensity of the symptoms.

For example, after being placed in an anxiety causing situation for a period of time, you may develop the condition of a stomach ulcer or gastritis. The recognition of the cause and effect relationship here may be blurred by the day to day variations in certain foods that you eat. Foods which aggravate the condition can get the blame. These foods are really only aggravations and not the underlying cause.

In a state of anxiety, your tendency or susceptibility to react to the events in your life anxiously will be a mostly constant state. This state will vary less from day to day than aggravating factors such as diet. Periods of high or low stress in your life will also have a parallel course to the intensity of your stomach symptoms but with less immediate results than your diet. Determining the underlying susceptibility requires you to honestly look within for your reactions to life and to not take an easier, more comfortable approach of blaming some outside factor like a spicy meal.

It is likely that in response to any type of stressful situation you will react in all three areas (mental, emotional and physical) at the same time but with varying intensities at each level. In laboratory medicine, your physical state of susceptibility can be more easily defined by measuring the various parameters of your immune system. The mental and emotional parameters are not as easily defined and quantified. A holistic assessment of all the types of reactions you make (symptoms) when a susceptibility is encountered helps find the most effective treatment. The closer the treatment matches all the manifestations of your reaction, the more complete and permanent will be the recovery.

There is a direct link between the symptoms you have and your susceptibilities. All the symptoms you have had at previous times in your life and all those you have now or will have in the future, represent one of your susceptibilities. In your life, you will develop a set of symptoms that is unique to you. This is based on the fact that you both have a unique set of susceptibilities and have your own individual experiences in life.

The body will not produce a symptom without cause. The nature of your susceptibilities carries equal importance with the inciting event that results in the production of a symptom. Keep your symptom in perspective. Symptoms are a secondary reaction of the body and not as the primary cause of your reaction. Symptoms should be seen as representing the consequence of your interaction with a unique set of variables. This reinforces the need for individualization in selecting the most curative treatment. *When you think of the symptoms and diseases you have, you can know that they represent your unique susceptibilities.*

Think of all the diseases in life that you do not have. All of these diseases and their symptoms represent **resistances.** You come into life with an individualized set of resistances. This set predetermines that you will not have a certain problem—epilepsy, for example. You may add certain diseases to the set of resistances you have when you fully recover from a stress that you previously were susceptible to. This represents, in my opinion, the purpose of healing and the essence of evolution available in your lifetime.

Your natural resistance is a separate quality from vitality and sensitivity. Disease resistance represents a state of health that is determined at a level beyond your conscious control. The behaviors you consciously choose will have an impact on the type and number of stresses you are exposed to. Whether you are susceptible or resistant to a particular stress is not of your conscious choosing. You can think of all the symptoms and diseases that you do not have now or have never had in the past, and know that those are your unique resistances.

Examining a common experience of healing may help you to understand the process of healing as a transformational one of going from a susceptible state into a resistant state. Healing occurs as a natural healing process of life.

The disease chicken pox works nicely to illustrate healing as going from a state of susceptibility to a state of resistance. Chicken pox is a common disease that many people have experienced and have some knowledge of. Chicken pox is widely known to be caused by a virus and nearly everyone who has chicken pox recovers naturally, with full resistance to further occurrences of chicken pox. You will usually gain full resistance following one exposure to the virus.

For the purposes of this example, let's assume that you are one of the majority of people who have had chicken pox as a normal childhood disease and recovered. By definition, then, we can say that you came into life susceptible to chicken pox. Though you came into life susceptible to chicken pox, you did not have chicken pox until life brought you a particular type of stress, in this case, the varicella virus that causes chicken pox.

Only when the susceptible person comes into contact with the virus, does he begin to demonstrate the symptoms of the disease we recognize as chicken pox. Under the power of his or her vitality, our patient will exhibit the symptoms of chicken pox for a time and then recover good health. During the process of producing the symptoms of chicken pox, the patient is undergoing a transformation. He is recovering or healing. He is changing his state of health, or evolving into a state resistant to the chicken pox virus. This transformative process begins only after contacting the virus. This transformation is brought about through the production of the symptoms of chicken pox. Prior to the encounter with the virus, these symptoms were not produced and this evolutionary process was not undertaken by the body.

The patient's vitality will determine the length and severity of symptoms that are necessary for him to complete this transformative healing process. We can, therefore, see correspondingly different courses of the disease in children of the same family, when chicken pox breaks out in a neighborhood. The end result will be the same for all those children. They will develop full resistance to future outbreaks of chicken pox. Most children will experience a typical case of chicken pox. A few will have natural resistance from birth and not have any susceptibility to the virus. A few will have such high vitality that they develop resistance with hardly any detectable symptoms of the disease. Rarely, one may be too ill to respond to the virus, due to the presence of a more serious disease, and have an "apparent" resistance.

The chicken pox example offers a demonstration of some of the underlying principles at work in healing. *Symptoms are an important part of the transformative potential inherent in life that healing represents.* The evidence indicates that your symptoms are the mechanism of healing. The definition of healing is being expanded to include a long-term process of transformation or evolution of your state of health from a condition of susceptibility (weakness) into a state of resistance (strength).

Symptoms and healing are being seen together as the process that allows you to gain from the experience of coming into contact with things that currently have power over you. *The balance of power shifts in healing.* Those things that used to negatively influence your state of health now come under your control. You are now able to have a healthy response to things that used to create an unhealthy response. This change represents a strengthening or evolution in your individual capabilities.

You can encounter many challenges to your health in life. This can include all challenges to your safety and comfort in life on the physical, mental or emotional level. You, fortunately, bring into life a certain amount of resistance to many things. Actually, if you look at the huge number of diseases that are possible, you are resistant to the vast majority.

You will encounter many types of substances or influences in life that cause no symptoms. These are perceived to be safe for you and will not create an immunologic or symptomatic response. This definition of safe means that you can encounter these stresses and not be overwhelmed by them. You will interpret and react to them in a resistant way. You can now use the occurrence of these events in your life to your advantage.

Those substances or influences, that are not recognized as safe, will have to be evaluated through experience and responded to. This defines or gives purpose to your symptoms as a learning experience, in response to what life offers. All that we might perceive as health challenges can then be redefined as having the potential to stimulate your evolutionary or transformative experience of life. From a physical standpoint, this concept defines the purpose and actions of your immune system.

This new definition of the purpose of your response to life is consistent with the earlier principles presented as part of energetic & holistic medicine. This definition is certainly consistent with seeing all of your symptoms as good things. This new awareness of the meaning of symptoms rests on your acceptance of the concept that symptoms lead to healing. The process of true healing occurs by transforming yourself into a resistant state. This is particularly easy to see in the example of an acute, infectious disease like chicken pox. The cause of symptoms in an acute case is apparent. You develop chicken pox after coming into contact with someone who already has chicken pox. It is a straight forward effect of passing on the virus. If you understand symptoms to represent a transformative process that takes us from susceptibility to resistance, it applies equally well in the case of chronic disease.

In the case of a chronic disease, a long time may have passed since the original cause has affected the patient. After a long time passes, the reactive symptoms will become the focus of everyone's attention. The shift of focus from cause to symptoms seems to be a natural occurrence unless the cause continues to be experienced and worsens the symptoms. Thoughts about susceptibility may not seem very relevant once the reactive symptoms have become established as the focus of concern and treatment.

Chronic diseases represent a growing problem. Why? There must be something important being missed in the way disease is evaluated and treated. With each chapter, your knowledge is increasing of how an alternative view of understanding the cause of a chronic disease may offer you more hope of recovering from them. *It is important to keep your focus on the importance of the initial cause of a disease process in order to have a complete recovery.* Your goal should be that living life and aging does not have to mean inevitable suffering. The stories of my patient's experiences of healing offer some evidence that this expectation is reasonable. The book "Remarkable Recoveries" is entirely dedicated to establishing the fact that recovery from serious disease and suffering is a reality.

The Law of Similars, as the natural healing law of our world, applies equally well to chronic disease as it does to acute disease. If you examine the Law of Similars, together with the concept of healing as transformation from susceptibility to resistance, you will find them to be completely compatible.

The two concepts seem to create a completely consistent circle of logic. *If symptoms have as their primary purpose your strengthening through healing, then giving you more of the very same energy as your symptoms will help you complete the healing process.* The combined power and simplicity of this logic are actually amazing. The logic of working with the body's healing efforts is verified by the healing results that are obtained. The character of these results demonstrate increased signs of good health, a decreased likelihood of recurrences, no side effects and the phenomenon of return of old symptoms. The quality of this result argues that the logic being demonstrated is substantial and real.

Your next question to examine is: does the concept of healing as a transformation from susceptibility to resistance prove to be consistent with the previously developed concept of all healing as self-healing?

The process of transforming a susceptibility into resistance is entirely an internal process. The chicken pox example illustrates that it does require a stimulus from outside of yourself to initiate the process. Once the stimulus is encountered, the healing process is entirely directed from within. The nature and the severity of the healing response will be individualized to each person. There are boundaries of similarity in the response to each particular type of stress. The factors that determine the ultimate result you obtain are unique to each individual (susceptibility, vitality, sensitivity and the type of treatment you receive).

The strength of the offending stimulus will be part of the equation determining your ability to respond. It is obviously different for chickenpox than a gunshot wound to the chest. Your vitality is equally important in determining the potential of your self-healing response. A very high vitality may account for a strong symptomatic response to a strong challenge in an area of high susceptibility. A high vitality may result in a weak symptomatic response to a weak challenge in an area of minimal susceptibility. As you can see, more than one variable has to be considered in evaluating the meaning of your symptomatic response.

The phenomenon of spontaneous remission and the placebo response, by definition, would lend support to the opinion that self-healing and the transformation of susceptibility are concepts consistent with one another. The placebo response and spontaneous remissions demonstrate that healing takes place by an internally controlled mechanism. By definition, no treatment has been in either case given or the treatment that was given had no expectation of being beneficial.

The historical record of patients experiencing a spontaneous remission is that they maintain their health and freedom from disease for long periods of time. The results of these cases may allow you to infer they have achieved a level of resistance or health that was not present previously. This area has probably never been studied thoroughly, and would be worthwhile research for our teaching institutions.

The concepts of healing as self-healing and the transformation of susceptibility have in common the understanding that in order to completely heal: you must deal with the cause of the problem. For a recovery to be defined as complete; healing should mandate that the treatment confers a reduced likelihood of future recurrences of the same problem.

A specific illness will usually have only one underlying cause or susceptibility as expressed in the healing process that the symptoms represent. An individual patient may experience some variations in their symptoms at different times. These variations can result from other factors being present that influence the initial susceptibility or a second susceptibility. Other factors besides the original cause of the symptoms may increase or decrease the patient's symptoms.

Treatments that are directed primarily at secondary symptoms, by working against the body (anti), may cut short the time period of the symptoms but may not necessarily complete the healing process with gaining full resistance. A recurrence of the same symptoms indicates the patient still has a need for more healing as their process of gaining complete resistance and transformed health.

Factors that increase your vitality would seem to have the potential to improve your chance of healing with resistance. Factors that decrease the magnitude of the stress encountered may also speed recovery, but not necessarily help the process of healing to acquire full resistance.

There are a number of factors that influence your healing result. It may be more important for expanding your understanding of the healing process to examine what is the underlying control mechanism of healing.

What is the mechanism controlling your healing process is a difficult question. Where would you say the direction comes from in controlling the process or sequence of events as you recover from an illness? The placebo response and cases of spontaneous remission shed light on the process of control in healing. I know surgeons like to think we have control of every facet of surgery. The internists often refer to the "management" of their patients as if they were in control. Certainly, doctors can have a strong influence on our patient's state of health, but I doubt we are as much in control as we like to think. Our greatest power is probably in modifying the intensity of external factors initiating your symptomatic response.

When you examine the question of what is the force or system that is in control of the healing process, it is hard to get away from the concept of a "vital force". This vital force can't be located easily in any system of the body. It does not seem to have a physical presence or an anatomical location. If you objectively look at the healing process, there must be a identifiable system of control that is precise and powerful.

Let me give you a simple example. Not too long ago, I was peeling apples, a little carelessly, and sliced off a part of the inside of my left index finger with the peeler. I can tell you that the part of my finger that I removed was certainly a viable part of my finger, and not just dead skin. It bled briskly and smarted like a typical open wound. The injury had reached the level of the blood vessels and nerves. It took several weeks for this wound to heal but when it did, the finger looked the same as it did before the injury. Initially there was a divot in the finger and with time, all the tissues that were lost recreated themselves. It was a little pink looking for a month or two but eventually you could not tell where the injury had been.

It is interesting to look at what happened with this minor injury. The healing process occurred without any conscious direction by me. The tissue that was lost was regenerated by my finger without a scar. Where is the blueprint for this type of information? The recovery process had a memory of what the nature of the tissue was prior to the injury and recreated the lost tissue. Your body has this ability to constantly regenerate itself in all tissues. All tissues have a rate of cell turnover. We continually replace our body tissues in an orderly manner that does not alter your function or structure. This has to be an organized and controlled process, but we have no evidence anatomically of where the control mechanism is.

The powerful capabilities of our healing system must have a very complex system of control. It is my impression that this is directed at the level of the body's subtle energy system. Your subtle energy system is that difficult to conceptualize system from Chinese medicine that includes concepts like "Chi" and "Essence". Hopefully, as the science of diagnostic electro-acupuncture advances, there will be better evidence available to quantify the actions of our energetic controls of health.

The mechanism by which your vital force continually perfects your state of health by utilizing the vast amounts of data available to it will likely stay a mystery for some time. The best approach for now is to learn the principles of healing indicated by the actions of your vital force and work with them instead of against them.

In order to understand healing at the energetic level, the meaning of the word susceptibility may need to be very encompassing. Your understanding of susceptibility can be enhanced by making other observations about the healing process. One observation is the **return of old symptoms** and another is the concept of a **constitutional remedy.** They may be the same thing, just looked at from the reference of different times in life—your past and your future.

When a patient is receiving a deeply-curative homeopathic remedy, in a strong potency, they may recreate symptoms from previous times in their life. Typical symptoms might be a rash, a hacking cough or an ankle pain that feels like an old sprain. The symptoms that are produced will appear and disappear under the healing influence of the remedy and no other treatment is usually necessary. The symptoms are often ones that are typically known to be treatable with the remedy being used.

The presumption is made in homeopathy that these previous symptoms are being called back from some memory bank in the tissues. It is thought that healing to the level of full resistance was not completed when the symptoms originally appeared in the past. The incomplete nature of healing may be due to a suppressive or purely symptomatic type of treatment being used. The patients will often be experiencing strong signs of overall improvement in their general health under treatment with the constitutional remedy when the previous symptoms reappear. A similar presumption is made that at the time the original symptoms occurred, the present remedy would have been the correct remedy to treat the previous condition.

The commonly observed phenomenon of return of old symptoms under homeopathic care raises a difficult to answer question. Do the current symptoms and the previous condition represent the same susceptibility, in light of the fact that the same energy (homeopathic remedy) will treat them? Looking at the concept of a constitutional remedy may shed more light on the question.

It is a goal in the treatment of most patients with the homeopathic system of medicine, to find what is called a constitutional remedy. This is especially important in the treatment of chronic diseases. The constitutional remedy is the one that best matches the totality of the patient's physical, mental and emotional symptoms at the present time and those symptoms that have appeared previously in their life.

The constitutional remedy will usually be the most deeply curative remedy for patients. The constitutional remedy has the ability to remove the greatest number of symptoms and improve many of the parameters of good health. Once this remedy has been discovered for a patient, it can be used in the future to treat new conditions. If the constitutional remedy is used over a long period of time, in slowly increasing potencies, the patient may experience a marked improvement in their health and not be prone to illness at all.

The concept of a constitutional remedy, together with the phenomenon of return of old symptoms, helps your understanding of susceptibility. One energy (homeopathic remedy) can treat symptoms in a patient in a number of different tissues or organ systems of the body. One remedy can treat a number of different symptoms at various times in the life of the patient. This is consistent with the holistic understanding of health.

All tissues will respond to a challenge according to the nature of the tissue that they are. Recall that the stomach and the knee are energetically related along the stomach meridian. They will both respond to a similar type of stress. The symptoms they produce will be quite different because of the very different type of tissues that they are. It is therefore possible for you to find one homeopathic remedy that is able to treat a variety of symptoms in the knee and stomach that may have occurred at different times in the health history of the patient.

There appears to be an energetic relationship between your current symptoms and symptoms that either have occurred in your past history or will occur in your future. This opens the possibility that an energetic treatment you do today can prevent you from having a similar or a different problem in the future. This possibility gives energetic & holistic medicine a measure of excitement and satisfaction beyond what you might get from a pharmaceutical approach.

Another common explanation used in homeopathy to interpret the results that are seen as patients heal is the concept of "**layers**". The layers concept has been developed to explain the results seen as people heal using remedies. In this concept, people are theorized to often have several different layers of susceptibility. Each layer represents a distinct potential for symptoms and energetic treatment. Each separate layer will be treatable with a specific remedy and represents its own distinct set of symptoms.

Many patients are likely to have several layers of symptoms. The patient will need a different remedy to treat the symptoms of each different layer. The remedy that relieves the symptoms of one layer usually will not remove the symptoms of other layers. A small minority of patients will be all one layer and one constitutional remedy will remove all of their symptoms. Most patients have one larger constitutional layer that includes most of their symptoms and usually the longest lasting ones. For this majority of patients, the other layers they have represent a distinct set of symptoms that the constitutional remedy will not relieve. This distinct layer represents a distinct susceptibility.

Prescribing remedies can be complicated when the patient's symptoms can be removed by more than one remedy. If each layer represents a different susceptibility, there must be some overlap of the energy of one susceptibility with another. This overlap of symptoms is reflected clinically in the occurrence of similar symptoms when you experience a cold or have hay fever. Your susceptibilities can also have similar traits. You can see this by comparing a susceptibility to two similar types of stress, such as irritability and anger. These two emotional states are both different and similar.

It is interesting to observe what happens when a layer is treated. In an acute situation, when the correct remedy is chosen, the symptoms may quickly subside and never return. In a chronic situation, as the potency of the correct remedy is repeated and raised in potency over time, the symptoms of that layer will be expressed less often and with less severity. Eventually the symptoms should disappear and only recur under the greatest of stresses.

This experience of energetic healing parallels our concept of susceptibility but gives the impression that full resistance may or may not be acquired after one contact with a stress. Energetic healing is thought to be working with the body and gives the impression that full resistance seems to be achieved in a step wise manner for some types of susceptibility.

This observation of step-wise healing has some similarity with our observations on the workings of the immune system's antigen-antibody response. The immune system requires some minimum threshold level of antigen be detected in order to initiate a response. Individual substances will have different thresholds of tolerance by the body before it reacts. Allergy desensitization shots use this principle in decreasing the reactions to allergens.

A constitutional remedy has the ability to produce a beneficial healing reaction over a long period of time in a person's life as well as the ability to treat a wide variety of symptoms. There is apparently something about the susceptibility associated with this particular unbalancing influence that requires a larger number of activations to achieve full resistance.

It is difficult to answer the question of how the constitutional remedy has an ability to recall old symptoms and resolve them. It might be that the old and new symptoms represent the same susceptibility now being expressed in different tissues. It may be that the symptoms represent somewhat different susceptibilities that have enough similarity or resonance with the energy of the constitutional remedy to respond to treatment.

You now have a little more evidence to answer the question of how the sequence of diseases in your life relate to another. This question relates directly to the nature of your susceptibilities. There are still questions about why you have the susceptibilities you do and what they represent. The answers to these questions are clinically relevant. *The more you can understand about your susceptibilities and your healing response to them, the better you can pick a curative treatment and stay healthy.*

These questions are practical ones for homeopathic practitioners. Some practitioners find success in their practice using a small number of remedies to treat most patients and conditions. They are called the polychrest prescribers. They use well known remedies with wide spheres of action in most cases and have success. Their experience indicates that the number of susceptibilities any individual might have is a small number.

Patients will exhibit a variety of symptoms in their expression of susceptibility over time. The patient's pattern of symptoms represents their individual personality and experiences. With the constitutional remedy you will see a healing response in various tissues at various times in their life. Variations result from individual differences in the types of stresses a person experiences in their life and the tissues that react to produce symptoms. Many of these individual differences would seem to have less importance than the more generalized effect of the homeopathic remedy according to the experience of the polychrest prescribers.

There is another group of homeopathic prescribers who like the challenge of knowing all 2000 homeopathic remedies and use a much wider variety of remedies. They also get good results in their patients. This group's experience would indicate there can be a large number of distinct susceptibility states that can be treated individually. There is no way to know if another remedy might also have produced a curative response in the patient. Once a patient responds to any remedy there is no way to undue the recovery and go back and see if another remedy could have worked as well or better.

Knowing the nature of your susceptibility has important bearing on understanding the nature of the cause of your disease state. It would be helpful to know what you are reacting to. When you have a more definite knowledge of what has triggered your susceptibility, the challenge of healing is more clearly defined. You can then work on strengthening your resistance to this type of challenge.

Being aware of your susceptibilities would speed up the process of transforming a susceptibility into a strength or resistance. The better defined is the challenge, the less likely it is you will venture into the wrong treatment and waste time and effort. This advantage would be helpful in shortening the tedious homeopathic process of working each individual case for the cause of their symptoms and the best matching remedy. *Discovering your susceptibility has relevance to your search for understanding the meaning of your symptoms.* It would be helpful in decreasing the time, expense and complexity that is involved in a holistic approach to the patient.

Dr. Reckeweg proposed an interesting concept in the 19th century that he called homotoxicology. He developed homotoxicology from observing recognizable patterns of disease that occurred in patients. This included patterns of disease progression as well as recovery. He observed that a patient might at first have an eczema problem and following a treatment that only repressed the symptoms, the patient might later develop asthma. If the asthma was also treated suppressively (anti), after a period of time, the patient might develop a colon cancer. When he was able to reverse the disease process with homotoxicology, he expected the asthma to return as the colon cancer was treated curatively. Similarly, the eczema would be expected to return following curative therapy for the asthma.

Dr. Reckeweg recognized a number of patterns of disease progression through different organ systems. In the modern day of specialization and short term studies, it would be hard to recognize disease patterns like this. Homotoxicology tends to indicate that the body can be responding to a single stress or susceptibility at various times with a completely different disease presentation. The body first responds to a challenge with a less vital organ system and produces less dangerous symptoms. Only when this expression is suppressed does the body move its response to a secondary, more vital organ system with a response that has a more powerful effect on the health.

If you have read this far into the book, your open mindedness and propensity for speculative thinking will, hopefully, allow you to proceed. Eastern philosophy has close ties to the Eastern system of medicine.

The Eastern concept of karma may coincide with this discussion of susceptibility. When a person comes into this life, he is understood to have a karmic contract with life to have certain experiences. These experiences have as their intention both learning and personal evolution. These experiences can at times be our most challenging stresses. Others may be equally joyful. Life is understood as being kind to you when it brings you the experiences that fulfill your karmic contract. It is offering you these karmic opportunities for your growth. The process may involve symptoms but your suffering is only required to stimulate your transformation. This is similar to the concept of symptoms being ultimately for your benefit.

It is implied in the karmic contract, that once you have mastered this challenge, the contract is void and life will stop bringing you these challenges. The symptoms will stop occurring once they have no further purpose to serve. The concept of a karmic contract seems consistent with the development of resistance through symptoms. This concept of karma reinforces our more optimistic view of symptoms. If you can work with yourself successfully to recover health, you may find it easier to maintain better health in the future. You may be able to more fully enjoy life through losing the limitations that susceptibility imposes on you.

I would propose that it may be reasonable to consider your healing process of going from susceptibility to resistance as the evolutionary opportunities of your life. However you see the debate between evolution and creation, there may be a process of evolution available to each person in their lifetime. Evolution may be more than just going from fish to monkeys over millennia. The stresses you encounter in your life are helping advance your evolution or transformation during this lifetime.

Your Healing Heart

Awareness

All Healing is Self-Healing

Law of Similars =
The Healing Law of Nature

Healing = Transforming
Susceptibility into Resistance

Vital Force = "The Big You"

The Disease of Fear

Acceptance

Changing Your Perception of Reality

Being Open-Minded to
Alternative Views of Reality

It's OK to Talk to Yourself
and Listen to Your Body

The Amazing Human Being

Western Medicine has Value
as a Healing System

Forgiveness

The Meaning of Symptoms and Disease

You're OK

Healing: The Never Ending Story
= Learning and Healing Through
Life's Opportunities and Challenges

Chapter 6

The Little You & The Big You

Holistic medicine makes sense mostly because you are holistic. Both the nature of your mechanism for self-healing and the purpose that is served by all of your symptoms appear to be holistic. No part of you is separate from the rest or is not completely integrated in serving these healing functions. Both the principle of self-healing and symptoms as healing appear to be universal in their application. The Law of Similars applies equally well to people and animals. This law of healing has been applied successfully for centuries and without a need for revision. These facts raise a very interesting question for your consideration next: What is the underlying control mechanism determining your state of health that allows the healing process to be orderly and to have remained the same without the need for change?

In order to answer this question, it will be necessary to explore the nature of the human being at a level beyond what we can observe as the physical, mental or emotional aspects. It will be necessary to consider evidence that is more experiential than experimental in order to understand this level of control of your health. It is not possible to have experimental evidence using human subjects in investigating this deeper level of control that ultimately determines your health. The science of subtle energy medicine may open up this in the future. Diagnostic electro-acupuncture and kinesiology may be tools used in the future to test out various hypotheses.

Experiential evidence can be scientifically valid when it meets the criterion of measurability, predictability, reproducibility and verifiability. Both my studies of historical systems of medicine and personal experiences observing patients heal themselves have led me to the initial conclusions presented to you in this chapter. They represent only anecdotal evidence. Case reports and the assumptions they indicate need to be verified by larger studies that can achieve statistical significance. Clinicians can only produce the best results possible within their capabilities and knowledge. The teaching institutions have to put these concepts to unbiased testing to get us closer to a complete understanding of your healing mechanism and clarify the factors determining your state of health.

I have found it comfortable for most patients; in an explanation of this level of control of their healing mechanism, to use the term the Big You and the little you. I strictly avoid a discussion of either politics or religion in the office. Discussing either area can tightly close down a mind and the patient will be limited in his ability to learn how to heal himself. The term vital force seems neutral when used with patients and works nearly as well. Patient education is assisted by giving non-confrontational names to the part of the human being that is beyond the ability of our mind or five senses to detect. The vital force represents the state that is clearly present during the condition of being alive and is clearly absent when the patient has expired.

Homeopathic medicine and Chinese medicine have always assumed the existence of an organizing "vital force" as a spirit-like force that controls a person's health beyond the level of our conscious control. This deeper level of control functions as a purely energetic system and represents the level where energetic medicine interacts with the patient. This concept is not recognized or utilized in western medicine as being a source of control that primarily determines your state of health.

The reader of this book is recommended to just look at this chapter as the author's own personal speculation. These opinions rest primarily on studies and experiences like those covered in the prior chapters. It will be helpful for readers to have at least some speculative foundation for understanding the principles that underlie the phenomenon of healing that we have been investigating. It is a consistent expression of human nature to desire an explanation for the events occurring in your life. These explanations can help form the basis for the actions you take in response to those events.

All students of healing are entitled to have their own opinions and hopefully you will find this discussion useful. Having some level of understanding about the controlling force behind the healing process can impart a sense of stability or predictability when you need to make decisions about your health. This stability will allow you to be more comfortable in the decisions you make relative to your health. There will always be choices. This chapter encompasses my own understanding of the set of circumstances that work to determine your state of health. These opinions are subject to being changed in the future as more experiences occur in my life or other studies are completed. I expect that to happen. I look forward to being exposed to and challenged by different interpretations of the meaning of healing by other students who have had the benefit of different experiences in their life.

In searching for the guiding force behind the process of healing, the answer needs to be consistent with your observations. The answer also has to be consistent with reality (even though a completely accurate awareness of reality is unknowable). The answer needs to be able to explain why what happened has occurred as well as be able to reliably predict the outcome of any actions you take to influence your state of health.

There are limits to your ability to understand all the forces of the world. This does not detract from their validity. Using the Law of Gravity as an example is helpful in appreciating the limits of our ability to understand all the forces that exist as a reality in the world.

No one would disagree with the reality that gravity exists. You constantly observe its actions and use it to predict the results of your actions in the future. It is a never-changing constant. The world would not exist as it is, if gravity was subject to variation. Gravity maintains the orbit of the earth around the sun. If the attractive force of gravity increased or decreased, the distance between the two planets would change and the world as you know it could not remain the same.

Interestingly, no one alive today has the slightest understanding of why gravity exists, or where the force of gravity comes from. It is not knowable at our current level of understanding. That doesn't mean it does not exist. It just means we don't know why or how.

Gravity, then, serves as a nice analogy for the force that controls your state of healing. Your force for healing is also a very subtle energy that is difficult to measure directly. The presence and actions of this healing force can only be inferred from making observations or measurements that represent its actions.

In order to illustrate the need for this discussion about the force controlling healing, and to show why it can be helpful, I am going to ask another question of you. This is a very challenging question.

In preparation for your answer, it will be helpful to remember the principles of healing that we have already established. First, you have explored the concept that all healing is self-healing. Second, you have studied the Law of Similars as our healing law of nature. Third, you have learned that all of your symptoms are good things and represent the healing actions of your body. In the last chapter you explored the concept of healing as a transformation from a condition of susceptibility to one of resistance.

Now I want you to consider this question with all of the previous concepts as background information. You want to develop an answer that is consistent with all the facts that have been presented. Your answer should be inclusive and consistent with all your experiences. Your answer should allow you to be able to predict the effects that will result from your behaviors. This should include all your thoughts and actions as behaviors that influence your state of health.

Remember that all your symptoms or diseases represent healing actions of the body. When you receive more energy that is the same as the energy of your symptoms, you will heal yourself. Remember all the diseases and symptoms that you do not have. Giving you the energy of those symptoms would not have any influence on your health. You already have full resistance to that set of unbalancing influences on the body. Remember that you produce symptoms holistically. All mental, emotional and physical symptoms are useful in finding the matching energy to heal you. Your healing will also occur holistically under the influence of the energy that best matches your state of health.

The question is: **How do you know to produce the exact set of symptoms that are the perfect ones to heal yourself?** How do you know to produce the specific set of symptoms that are the best ones to facilitate your transformation from a state of susceptibility into a more evolved state of resistance?

Your ability to direct this level of control of your state of health is obviously beyond the capabilities of the conscious mind. The facts indicate that this capability is a universal phenomenon of the human being. Whatever evidence you use to answer this question will have to be individually derived from your observations of healing and what you have been taught. How close anyone's answer to this question is to the truth of the reality of healing can be measured by two criterion: one, the ability of their answer to explain the cause and effect relationship observed between all the influences on their health and the resultant changes in their health, and second, their answer's ability to accurately predict the outcome of various treatments.

After proposing this puzzling question to you, I feel obligated to give you my best answer, based upon the knowledge available to me in the year 2005. In order to answer this question, I will need to divide the human being into two different pieces. I will call one piece the little you and the other piece the Big You.

By my definition, the little you is all that you are able to know of yourself and your life using your five senses and your conscious mind. Now that is a lot, and is how you would normally be aware of yourself and the world around us.

It is my contention, that in the creation of the human being, there has been a design limitation included in the human being at the level of the little you. This design limitation makes it impossible for you to know, at the level of the conscious mind and the five senses, what are the perfect set of symptoms to produce that will improve your health. That design limitation is in the mind.

The design limitation inherent in your conscious mind is that you are only able to think of one thought at a time. You may be able to rapidly have one thought after another but you will not be able to simultaneously have fifty or fifty thousand thoughts at the same time. Or, at least, you would be the first person I have met with that capability. This is the important limitation that makes it impossible to know, with your conscious mind, what symptoms are best for you. The human being is still a great thing at this level but just not capable of consciously directing its own healing process.

Let me now introduce you to that other part of yourself, the piece I call the Big You. It is quite an amazing thing, this Big You. It has always been a part of you and always will be a part of you. As you learn of it, you should be thoroughly impressed by yourself and your capabilities. The human being is quite an amazing creation. The Big You is capable of doing trillions of things at the same time and that may be a conservative estimate.

At the level of the Big You, you are able to have an incredible view of yourself and your life. It is from this view that there is a perfect logic to produce the state of health and the exact symptoms that are best for you. The vision that you have at the Big You level includes two quite grand views. One view is the ability to see every weakness (susceptibility) and strength (resistance) that you have. You are also able to see exactly what proportion of strength or weakness you have in every facet of your being (physically, mentally and emotionally). All the knowledge of exactly who you are is included in this view of your self and is available for use in creating your state of health.

In addition to having this incredible amount of data available on who you are at the Big You level, you have another type of vision available that helps you determine the perfect symptoms to produce in order to heal. Second, at the Big You level you are simultaneously able to see every event that has ever occurred in your life, from the moment of conception up until the present moment. Both of these views are available to you at all times on the Big You level. It is from this precise knowledge of both who you are and all the events that have occurred in your life, that you apply perfect logic in producing the exact set of symptoms that allow you to heal and raise your state of health towards comfort and joy. With this expanded view of who you are, you should be quite rightly impressed by yourself and the amazing creations that we all are.

This is a good place to stop any further speculation into why things are as you experience them. It is likely impossible to go beyond this level of understanding as to why you have the state of health that you do. It is of little practical importance to know why this particular functional design of the human being has been created as long as it can be used reliably to accomplish healing. The design that I have proposed is workable and seems to fit the purposes of this study of healing and this theory is consistent with all the information I have gathered in studying various therapeutic systems of medicine.

It may be of some value to give you further examples of the amazing capabilities of the Big You and the state of being human that you are experiencing. I will offer three examples from your everyday experiences in life. Keep in mind with these examples, the influences that your Big You is exerting in continually perfecting your state of health. This is true no matter who you are by nature and what circumstances are imposed upon you by the world or your conscious mind.

For the first example, I would like you to think back to the last meal that you have eaten. That meal is now providing you the energy that you expend in living your life. The components of that meal will provide the substances you use to replace and replenish the physical body that you have. Remember, every minute about 10,000 new cells are created to replace old cells in your body. This is done in an orderly process that neither has nor requires any conscious input.

You may have consciously decided what to eat in the last meal that you had, but the Big You takes over from there. The Big You will direct the process of breaking that food down into its individual molecules to make them available for use in the body. You will not need to have any conscious input into that process. Once the process of digesting your meal has broken the food down to its individual molecules, you will then look at each molecule and make a decision. You will decide which molecules are the good ones to take in and become part of who you are and which molecules are not good for you and you will let these ones just pass right through. In this first example, you can get an idea of the huge number of things that the Big You is capable of doing simultaneously.

For the next example, I would like you to consider the last breath that you took. There is probably a good chance that the Big You was also in the driver's seat in this case. You can override the Big You and choose when to breathe but it will not as likely be the best choice to meet your needs. If you error on the side of breathing too fast or too slow, the Big You will take over and put the conscious mind to rest and take over your respiratory rate to recover a more ideal rate of breathing.

The Big You determines your rate of breathing in a way that maintains the necessary gases in your lungs at an ideal level. It then directs each one of those gases to every cell of your body in just the right concentrations and at exactly the right time. Again, you don't have to be consciously burdened by getting any gas to any cell in the right amount or at the right time.

Hopefully, you will find this last example quite impressive in understanding just how amazing a system you have in perfecting your state of health at all times. Your heartbeat is an interesting example of this reality. It is known that if you measure the beat-to-beat interval of the heart down to a hundredth of a second, you will find that the beat-to-beat interval is never exactly even. With every heartbeat the Big You varies the rate to exactly meet the ever-changing needs of your body. When your heart beats, before it beats again, the Big You will assess the needs and circumstances of every cell of the body. It is able to do this through the energy information system of the body, the meridians of Chinese medicine. These energy communication lines can conduct much greater amounts of information and at a much more rapid pace than the physiologic control system in the blood.

The reality of this inclusive system of control perfecting your health is brought home in one striking reality. That is; the cardiologists have found the best predictor of the imminent end of life that is known is when the beat-to-beat interval of the heart is measured to be exactly regular. That is because you continuously maintain this ability to perfect your health, based on the needs and circumstances of every cell of your body, up until the very end of your life. This capability is reflected in your heartbeat. Life will not extend very long after the loss of this capability of your heart to perfectly adapt to all the influences on your health.

These examples allow you to have more insight into the amazing capabilities you are utilizing to perfect your state of health at all times. There are different levels of control of your health. You have a conscious level of control with the ability to make decisions that have bearing on your health. The level of control that is the basis of western medicine also plays a vital role in stabilizing your health. This system is represented by your gross anatomy and physiology and is typically evaluated by measuring levels of various components in the blood. There is also another level of control that works in your best interests to improve your health. I have termed that level as the Big You.

These examples tend to indicate that there is a vital force that functions with its own system of logic and principles. The actions of the vital force imply that there is an evolutionary intention to the specific symptoms you experience in life. It seems to me, that it is beyond doubt that there must be a logical force controlling our reactions to life and these reactions allow us to benefit from the experiences that life brings us. The resultant actions of this process resemble the principles of natural selection proposed by Darwin but they indicate involvement of the vital force in determining the results. Natural selection appears to be a valid observation of the mechanism of evolution but an organizing force is directing the evolutionary process.

You would be overlooking a very powerful aspect of yourself to limit your thinking to only the perceptions of your conscious awareness as determining your health. Patients constantly provide their doctors with reinforcement of this principle. Melinda provides a good example of the limitations of perception. For all that you might see and know of Melinda, you would certainly think that she is a picture of good health. She is a bright, smiling, attractive young woman with a nice family and a stable job. But, Melinda has psoriatic arthritis.

It always presents an interesting question when people who would seem to have all the right things in life develop a chronic disease. She had been evaluated and treated by both rheumatologists and dermatologists but continued to have symptoms and need treatment. Her doctors did not expect that she would completely recover from her disease and be able to discontinue treatment. There was no way for them to see the cause of her disease through their examinations or blood tests. It was their understanding that she had a chronic disease and would always need some form of treatment. There was also no way for them to treat the cause of her disease by using drugs for her treatment. Only a thorough, holistic assessment of all the implications of her symptoms could help her heal herself.

There was a reason for her symptoms but it could not be detected when looked at with the perspective of the little you level. Only at the level of understanding available to the Big You would the perfectly logical reasons for her disease be known. Once the healing intention of the Big You is recognized for what it is, its purpose can be served by working in conjunction with the symptoms.

The Big You recognized her new treatment (homeopathic) as being consistent with the intention of her symptoms and promptly directed a complete reversal of all her symptoms—both the psoriasis and the arthritis. The X-Rays and blood tests confirmed what she saw and felt. Her health had returned to completely normal. Both the process of creating her disease and its healing were directed by her Big You.

Bringing this process to the level of the patient's conscious awareness helps make the process satisfying and efficient but it does not direct or control the process. That level of control is just not designed into our conscious awareness. The value of bringing the cause of her disease into her awareness is in the prevention of future diseases.

The deeper answer to the pivotal question of what is determining your present state of health and what is your potential for growth and recovery of better health does have practical applications. Melinda's new state of vibrant health confirms the value of seeking out a deeper level of understanding and treating the cause of your symptoms. If there is a working logic to healing, it certainly seems more reasonable to swim with the flow of logic than to fight against the tide. If you go with the flow you are more likely to make faster progress in the direction of ease. Going against the flow may more likely take you in the direction of disease.

To make progress, or evolve, we are going to need some stress or turbulence in the flow. Do not be as antagonistic towards the stresses and challenges that come to you in life. Listening to your body will point you in the direction of profiting from the experiences. You will have a choice in treatments. You can work with the body or against it. At least be consistent in the logic you apply and honest in evaluating the results you get. Your speed of growth in health or evolution is at stake.

Transforming from susceptibility to resistance requires a stimulus. Life will continue to bring you the opportunities to grow, your job is to notice if you are profiting from them. Once you have learned how to profit from a system of logic, it gets easier to learn subsequent lessons. Practice thinking holistically in considering the type of events you are reacting to and holistically in the type of secondary reactions you are producing. Remember that for an acute problem it will be easier to see the cause. For a chronic condition, the cause may be more difficult to uncover, as it is more remote in time.

Your Healing Heart

Awareness

All Healing is Self-Healing

Law of Similars =
The Healing Law of Nature

Healing = Transforming
Susceptibility into Resistance

Vital Force = "The Big You"

The Disease of Fear

Acceptance

Changing Your Perception of Reality

Being Open-Minded to
Alternative Views of Reality

It's OK to Talk to Yourself
and Listen to Your Body

The Amazing Human Being

Western Medicine has Value
as a Healing System

Forgiveness

The Meaning of Symptoms and Disease

You're OK

Healing: The Never Ending Story
= Learning and Healing Through
Life's Opportunities and Challenges

Chapter 7

The Amazing Human Being

I would like to suggest that you clearly deserve to think of yourself as a truly amazing creation. The facts support this reality. It is quite appropriate that you be impressed by yourself. The purpose of this chapter is to explore further your amazing potential to heal. As you become aware of just how amazing your abilities to heal are and recognize that you are constantly producing the perfect symptoms to heal yourself, this awareness can be used to even further improve your health. Not everyone will want to delve into a study of their energetic anatomy or physiology, but if you have a persistent symptom that you can't seem to get rid of, this information may then become useful in finding a solution.

The previous chapters were intended to give you some insight into the natural process of healing that is available to you. The intention was for you to develop a deeper understanding about the meaning of your symptoms and the healing purpose they are serving.

Due to their uncomfortable nature, it would at first glance seem your symptoms and diseases have an inherently negative influence on your life. To understand the reason for the existence of your symptoms, it will be helpful to take a holistic view of yourself. Viewing the physical, mental and emotional ramifications that your symptoms are having on your life will give you a far more accurate interpretation of the reasons for their presence.

It is helpful if you can try and understand how your energetic systems control your health. This understanding will provide you a better working knowledge of the reasons for your current state of health and the mechanisms that are available to improve your health. The complexity and the amount of information that you are utilizing to perfect your health, at all times, is an astounding realization. It will require an open mind just to conceptualize the vast system of energetic physiology that you are making use of in determining your state of health.

It is important to keep a clear distinction in your mind between the two physiologic control systems that you utilize to determine your state of health. In energetic medicine these two systems are understood to always be working together to perfect your state of health. You produce your symptoms and your current state of health based upon your innate characteristics and the circumstances that have occurred or are occurring in your life. You have one control system that works at the level of gross physiology and anatomy. This level of control primarily provides stability to your health. You have a second system of control at the subtle energy level. Your subtle energy system primarily provides flexibility and capability to the process of determining your state of health.

From having been exposed to the paradigm of western medicine, you are more likely to be familiar with the functions and measurements of the control system that involves gross anatomy and physiology. This system characteristically looks at functions like regulation of the heartbeat (EEG) and uses measurements in the blood to determine the state of an organ's function (such as the levels of blood sugar or thyroid hormone). Most of these functions will be relatively stable over time. These tests measure the functioning of various tissues of the body to produce a secondary symptomatic response to what ever circumstances have caused the whole person to respond.

Based upon the principles outlined in previous chapters, your second level of control is understood to work at the subtle energy level and characterizes the actions of your "vital force". The working mechanism of your vital force, for the purpose of this discussion, will be considered to be your subtle energy system.

It is possible to see some differences and some similarities between the functioning of your gross and subtle energy systems. The most obvious difference between the energetic forces associated with the gross and subtle system is one of amplitude. A second difference is apparent in the anatomy of each system's conduction mechanism.

Several examples of the energetic component of your gross system of physiologic control are quite well known. These forces can be measured in millivolts or milliamps and are well recognized to control the function of your heart, brain and muscles. Measurements of their activity have been standardized for many years as the electrocardiogram (EKG), electroencephalogram (EEG) or electro-myogram (EMG). Both your heart and brain have well described conduction pathways for the electrical energies that control important function of your body.

Your subtle energy system is equally important for the healthy functioning of your mind and body and just as real as the more familiar system of gross energetic controls. The subtle energy system is more difficult to measure because it operates at the level of nanoamperes. Only recently has equipment been developed with suitable sensitivity and signal to noise filter ratios to reliably and objectively measure the level of energy in your subtle energy system.

Now that the level of energy in the subtle energy system can be measured, it is possible to make better evaluations and assessments of the functional controls associated with this level. The anatomy of the energetic conduction pathways of the subtle energy level of control has been best described by Dr. Pischinger in his work "Matrix Regulation". Dr. Pischinger details the anatomy and physiology of the system of mesenchymal communication and regulation. This communication mechanism connects every individual cell of the body to every other cell. It delineates the communication system that allows the whole person to be in touch with every cell as well. This communication system allows you to maintain the perfect holistic response to all influences that can impact your health.

Your subtle energy system is in constant communication with every cell of your body through an elaborate energy information system. The communication pathways are located in the ionic fluids of the extracellular spaces of the body. The speed at which information can be transmitted through this ionic medium is not limited by cellular membrane depolarization, as is the case in the mechanism of energy transmission used by your gross physiology. This allows the transfer of huge amounts of information along these pathways at very high rates of speed. Your subtle energy system is more comparable to the mechanism of information transfer that you are familiar with in the fiber optic cables of television or telephone communication.

Your subtle energy system is capable of handling the huge amounts of information necessary to holistically integrate the functions of every cell of the body. The subtle energy system allows you to integrate all the various information sources that have an influence on you in this world. The subtle energy system allows you to monitor all incoming stimuli from the visual, auditory, tactile and positional senses. There are potentially many other less obvious forms of energy or information that you are also monitoring. It would be beyond the purpose of this book to go into the science of subtle energy medicine in any greater detail, but suffice it to say, that technology is now bringing this area from the theoretical to the observable.

There are several areas worth exploring that can help you understand the workings of the subtle energy system and its control of your health. *One,* you need to get an idea of the magnitude of information that this system is taking advantage of at all times. *Two,* you need some awareness of the speed at which your subtle energy system is able to process all the information that comes from your own tissues and your surrounding environment. *Three,* you need to consider the types of influences that can affect your health and the importance of each one. *Four,* you need to consider the sequence of changes you observe in your health. By observing a pattern of when you develop symptoms in life following the occurrence of similar types of stresses, his observation will lead you to knowing one of your susceptibilities in life. *Five,* you will want to learn what exceptional demonstrations of healing can teach you about your own potential to heal.

It is somewhat staggering to consider the amount of information that your subtle information system is able to handle at any one time. From our discussion of The Big You, it appears that you have an enormous amount of information that is constantly being used to determine your state of health. This includes all the information contained in prior events in your life as well as all the information that goes into making up your individual characteristics and susceptibilities.

Your subtle information system is aware of the needs, status and circumstances presenting to every cell of the body. It controls the functioning of the body's repair process following all injuries (the cut finger example) and continually removes and replaces the cells of all the tissues of the body in an organized manner.

You are monitoring not only all the interior circumstances of your body, but you are responding to all influences from the external environment. A constant state of homeostasis is maintained. The best available use of and response to the energies that make up your environment will be continually maintained.

Your subtle energy system gives you a wide range of capabilities to adapt to the world and make the best use of all the information and substances the world provides you (the digestion example). Your healing or transformative potential, in response to the experiences in your life, would seem to have an almost unlimited number of possibilities. Through its control of the grosser physiologic functions, the subtle energy system insures your stability and comfort with the result that life is more secure and enjoyable. Considering the amount of information that is being processed, these systems work together with quite amazing proficiency. When both systems are working harmoniously for your benefit, your life will be long and you will have the potential to be quite comfortable and prolific.

Your vision affords an interesting example of the workings of your subtle energy system. Your eyes have a continuous wide field of view that takes in huge amounts of data and relays it into your "awareness". You have an elaborate filtering mechanism that is continually determining what part of this incoming data is appropriate for the attention of your conscious awareness.

Only a small part of the total data being received by your eyes is brought to the level of your conscious awareness. The rest of the information is being received but filtered to the level of the unconscious awareness. It has been demonstrated in forensic uses of hypnosis that data can be retrieved from your "extra-conscious" awareness that was never part of your conscious awareness. This data is stored in a memory bank that is a part of your awareness at some level outside of your conscious awareness or recall.

This ability gives you some appreciation for the amazing capability of processing and prioritizing incoming information that you have inherently as a human being. *It is quite amazing to considering the many types of physical information you are taking in at all times, as well as your feelings and thoughts, Your ability to filter them in an efficient way that maintains your health at an optimal and stable state is equally amazing.*

The speed at which you are able to conduct information in the subtle energy system and the speed at which you can determine the appropriate response to that information can not be measured. With diagnostic electro-acupuncture measurements, there is no delay between the introduction of a stimulus into the body and the measurement of your response to it. It seems to occur instantly. The speed is something akin to the speed of sound or light, which is just too fast for your conscious awareness to detect the response time. You have one heck of a high speed processor on board, but that is a necessary part of the design to function efficiently.

In considering what types of things will have an influence on your health and your capability of detecting them; you again need to take a very broad perspective. You have just been introduced to the concept that you are aware of countless pieces of information at any moment. All of this information can have an influence on your state of health. Why certain types of information will have more profound effects on your health is a more interesting question. It relates to the concept of susceptibility and to your potential for transformation or evolution during this lifetime.

When you encounter a stress, you will respond by producing the appropriate symptoms. This occurs whether your awareness of the influences on yourself is at the conscious or extra-conscious level. The sum of these influences and the resultant symptoms together define your current state of health.

At a level beyond the awareness of the little you, a decision or judgment is made to produce the ideal response. When you respond, the type of response and the intensity of your response will be determined by criterion that only can be defined by a somewhat illusive concept like the "vital force".

Clearly, an intelligent force is deciding upon the state you are experiencing as your state of health. Due to the limitations previously outlined as inherent in the conscious awareness of the little you, it is not possible for you to experience the workings of the vital force. At most, you are left with a grasp of the concept that an intelligent organizing force exists to constantly produce your ideal state of health.

The appearance of symptoms—as the reactive response of the vital force—can be used as an indication that a precipitating event in your life represents one of your susceptibilities. Encountering this susceptibility caused the vital force to initiate a symptomatic reaction. Your response indicates that this particular susceptibility has been prioritized to have significance for you in your overall process of evolution.

This brings you to the fourth area for consideration. *As you are able to pair your symptoms with events in your life that preceded their occurrence, you have the mechanism available to understand and work with your own vital force.* As you can observe the chronology of events in your entire life and the subsequent reactions to them, patterns may become apparent. You may be able to recognize those susceptibilities that carry the greatest importance for yourself. Observing this cause and effect time-line in your life can lead you to an important level of awareness. This awareness affords you the possibility of actually participating in your own process of transformation to optimal health.

When the little you and the Big You recognize and are reading from the same script, your current challenges can be most efficiently overcome and the severity and duration of your future challenges minimized. I do not feel that this is an overly optimistic view of reality but that it is based upon experience with scientific principles of healing.

Just to add to the potential speculation, it might be interesting to look at the holographic characteristics that human beings seem to possess. From ancient times, Chinese medicine has utilized the concept that any part of the body can represent the whole. In Chinese medicine the whole body can be treated by treating an isolated individual part of the body. The diagnosis of a condition in a remote part of the body can be made by observing changes in another location. This has proved itself to be true in a number of different applications over the centuries. Your holographic nature has resulted in the development of the fields of iridology, pulse diagnosis, palmistry, ear acupuncture, tongue diagnosis and reflexology.

Much of our modern day science is corroborating the wisdom of ancient systems of medicine. In order to understand healing, you might be best served by keeping a balance between reverence and skepticism towards traditional medical practices. Do not just simply reject something because it can't be substantiated or tested by analytical science. The "Chi" of Chinese medicine always seemed very imaginative to me until it became measurable with electro-acupuncture equipment.

An interesting modern day experience with the holographic nature of the human being is evident in the science of cloning. With cloning, a new complete individual is produced from a single starting cell that is separate from the natural reproductive process. Interestingly, the breakthrough that made cloning possible was the discovery of the exact conditions of an energetic force field that was applied to the initial cells. This specific energy could trigger the cell to initiate the process of recreating the entire animal from which the original cell came. Other criterion need to be met that will insure the survival of the cell, but the initiating event that starts the process is energetic.

From the perspective of yourself as an amazing human being, it will be good to go back and revisit the definition of healing and explore some examples. Healing or health can be defined as a state of freedom from the perspective of energetic and holistic medicine. In a state of disease you will experience limitations in your freedom and in a state of health you will have more freedom.

The specific freedom associated with health is the freedom to make choices in your reactions to the events occurring in your life. The main question to be answered is who is in control. When an event occurs in your life, does it control you or are you in control of your response to that event? The answer to this question will determine the extent of your freedom and the extent of your health. Healing represents a shift in the balance of power towards yourself in the control of your response to the events occurring in your life.

When certain events occur in your life and in your response to them, you can only react one way; you will ultimately trend towards the direction of disease. In this situation, the event has the power to control you. *When you lack the freedom to choose your response to a challenging event in life, this state of limitation will tend to take you in the direction of disease. The symptoms you then produce as your disease response represents the transformative process of being able to achieve control or power over this susceptibility.* Particularly, where your one available reaction to a type of event is a negative one (such as fear, anger or sadness), the occurrence of this type of event will lead to the production of symptoms and disease.

In the opposite case, where you have the freedom to choose among a variety of responses to a type of event occurring in your life, these type of events will not lead to the production of diseases. These are the personal characteristics that represent your strengths or resistances. In these situations, you have power and control over yourself and your responses to these events.

For an example of the situation where a person has limited freedom to choose their reactions to life, consider a case of road rage. These are the people you read about in the news, where somebody cuts them off in traffic, and they want to kill the other driver. Now that is certainly not a healthy response to an event occurring in your life and can lead to a lot of problems. Who is in control in this situation? Certainly not the road rage person. He has lost control and gives the power over his actions to the person cutting him off in traffic. The driver that cut him off determined his response state. He did not have the freedom to choose another response.

Now, how can the road rage driver get help to recover his power? He needs to gain the freedom to choose a healthier response from among the wider array of more healthy responses than road rage. Applying the Law of Similars can help. The homeopathic practitioner will need to give the road rage driver the homeopathic form of a substance that is known to be able to cause a rage response when given in its material form to anyone. The homeopathic forms of this substance will antidote the rage behavior. Under the influence of this homeopathic remedy the road rage driver will then have the experience of driving down the road and when someone cuts him off, he can choose a healthier response.

After driving a time under the healing influence of more of the same energy as his prior rage response, the road rage driver will have a number of experiences with varying, healthier responses to being cut off in traffic. These experiences will afford him the opportunity to learn of his ability to have more than one response to being cut off in traffic. This growth, available through learning by experience, will become a permanent change with time. He will develop the freedom and empowerment to choose a healthier response to life. He will not be as controlled by events outside himself. This transformation allows him to eventually have no further need for the homeopathic remedy. He can maintain his own freedom and power to make healthier choices in his behaviors. His freedom can eventually even include being free of the need for further treatment with homeopathic remedies. True healing creates no dependency upon the treatment.

Jay is an eight year old boy and demonstrates the concept of true healing and its significance quite well. He was experiencing some significant troubles in life both at home and at school. Jay was labeled as ADD and ODD (oppositional defiant disorder) with some sociopathic tendencies. He is a bright child but applied his abilities to all the wrong things. He was making a lot of bad choices with his behaviors in life. He and everyone around him were suffering the negative consequences. He was failing in school. He was a compulsive liar. He frequently got into fights and quarrels with other children and adults. He would steal things from others and from stores. He liked to light fires and even set his own house on fire during the day when his family was home.

Jay had been strongly medicated to control his behaviors and this worked well for the safety and happiness of everyone else around him, but it turned Jay into a veritable blob of inactivity. If the drugs were discontinued, all the previous behaviors returned. The drugs could have no lasting effect on whatever was the cause of his inappropriate behavior.

Drugs just made the rest of the world happier with Jay, but he was not fundamentally helped in any way. It turns out that there is a substance in our natural world that can cause these sorts of bad behaviors. It is the venom of the tarantula spider.

When Jay started to receive the homeopathic form of the venom, his behaviors started to improve. His previous drugs could be tapered down and discontinued after a few months and he continued to be able to control his behavior and apply his above average intelligence in a more constructive way. Jay is making quite a transition towards health and the freedom to make the healthier choices that holistic health entails.

Jay's experience raises an interesting question. Before receiving homeopathic treatment, he was labeled as a bad kid due to his many bad behaviors. After treatment, he now seems to be a good kid. It may be more accurate to say that he is just a person who is now having a different, healthier experience in his life. He will always be the same person, just exhibiting different states of who he is. It is still helpful to use good and bad labels in life to identify things, but you need to keep in mind that transformation through healing is always a possibility. This is especially true of behaviors that originate in the mental and emotional aspects of who you are.

It seems appropriate to end this chapter on your study of the amazing human being by revisiting those cases that demonstrate exceptional healing. Your astounding potential for healing has been demonstrated by Bill and similar accounts of people experiencing spontaneous remissions of all kinds of diseases. The universal nature of the placebo response also demonstrates that your healing ability covers every possible symptoms or condition that you may develop. All of these examples are useful in demonstrating the innate ability to heal that you and everyone else has as a natural birth right.

In order to investigate all of the possibilities of healing and be able to interpret the significance they can illustrate about the mechanisms of healing, it may be instructive to next investigate the phenomenon of faith healing. Nearly miraculous cases of faith healing have been reported over time starting with raising Lazarus from the dead and continuing up till the present day. Many cases and patterns of cases have been well documented.

The modern medical literature has published double-blinded controlled studies that have shown a statistically significant beneficial effect of prayer in the treatment of patients. Healing by prayer has been researched, published and is accepted by the scientific community. The healing effects of prayer have been demonstrated both in the hands-on situation and in selected cases where the healing has been done from a long distance away.

Since faith healing appears to be a reality that is widely available, it offers some potential for understanding the healing process. There are at the present time a fair number of people professing to have the ability to heal and are offering their services. I would like to share my observations with you on what appears to be common factors in the experience of these healers. It may add to your appreciation for how amazing all people are.

It is my impression that all people have an ability to be healers. This skill appears to be one that can be practiced and will become more proficient through practice. This opinion is based upon the premise that A Supreme Being is the universal healing force that is responsible for all healing that occurs. Some degree of faith is helpful for this type of healing to occur. Not all requests for healing or attempts to heal are successful. Certain requirements must be necessary for successful healing through prayer to be achieved.

Some requirements for success in faith healing are easier to define than others. It seems that there are at least three common factors needed for a successful outcome: One, the belief of the healer that healing can or should occur. Two, the belief of the person to be healed that their healing is possible or that they are worthy of being healed. Three, the healing serves the highest purposes for all the participants involved in the healing as discerned by the infinite wisdom of God.

It is important to understand that symptoms and diseases serve a purpose in the transformative experience of life. It would not necessarily be a negative thing for an attempt at faith healing to be unsuccessful. The purpose that the disease is serving may be greater that the purpose that would be accomplished by its being healed at the present time or healed in this way. The potential factors that go into the creation of a disease state can be far beyond the ability of the healer's or the person-to-be-healed's conscious awareness.

After taking a couple of instructional courses in healing and doing some related reading, I experimented with healing friends and family. I was able to verify, to my own satisfaction, that healing is an inherent ability that all people share. I had no intention of becoming a healer or felt a particular calling to it, but thought it was an interesting tool for physicians to be aware of.

I do not think alternatives like healing by prayer or spontaneous remissions should make the medical profession defensive. My experiences with faith healing left me with reverence for the healing wisdom and power of God. I am somewhat cautious with its proper use in the hands of people that may mean well but are unaware of all the factors involved in creating or healing a disease state.

My wife was my most frequent subject of these experiments and teacher in the process of investigating faith healing. My wife is a physician also and a trained observer of the phenomenon of medicine. She is healthy but driven to overwork like many physicians and subject to the secondary ailments that come from fatigue. We found it was not difficult at all to relieve her of the symptoms associated with fatigue by a simple focusing of healing attention on the condition and she could receive prompt and satisfactory results.

The ease of being able to relieve minor complaints with various healing techniques, either hands-on or remotely, led to it being required more frequently. This seemingly miraculous correction for the abuses of excessive work would allow my wife to extend herself even further in her work. It is for these reasons that I think even some caution needs to be taken in the appropriateness of the forgiving healing process that God makes available to us. God has given people this ability to heal others and it should be explored and utilized as the gift that it is. Since it comes from God it must have an inherently good effect and purpose. The intent is likely not the self aggrandizement or enriched ego of the healer. Neither should the one receiving the gift of healing not be appreciative of the renewal they have been granted and be unchanged or unaffected in their future behaviors and choice they make in life.

The last healing that we attempted rattled my perception of reality enough that I decided I had learned all I wanted to from these experiences. I had to leave early one morning for surgery and as I was leaving my wife told me that she was acutely ill and felt terrible. She had gone to bed fine but awoke too ill to get out of bed. She had a lot of important work that day and was feeling too terrible to do anything. I told her to stay in bed and that I would call her office later in the morning and cancel her patients. After leaving, I had a short time before surgery to try another experiment in healing. I sat down and focused all my attention on her and set an intention for her recovery. This lasted about five minutes and then I went to surgery.

I called my wife's office some time later to tell them to cancel her patients and was startled to hear that she was at work and fine. She later relayed to me this bizarre story of lying in bed and seeing me enter the room and walk over and sit down on the bed next to her. She said that I took her head in my hands and told her to open her mouth. I told her that I would breathe in her mouth and she would be fine. She objected because it was likely to make me sick as well but consented as I reassured her that all would be fine. After receiving this breath, I left and she slept for about fifteen minutes and awoke feeling just fine.

When my wife told me the story, I had not ever heard of anything quite this bizarre. I was sitting still in another location focusing my intention in a completely undefined way. Who or what she physically saw come into the room is impossible to say. She was convinced that it was me. This experience indicates that healing is possible through mechanisms that there will be no possible way to understand or even what is real or how such things can occur.

It is my feeling that the correct place for medical practitioners is in evaluating the mechanism and the effects of faith healing. I feel it is better to leave faith healing in the hands of the religious community. The principles outlined in this book are outlines for the scientific practice of medicine. An important principle of energetic medicine is that all healing is self-healing and these Divine healings represent an as yet unknown mechanism of healing.

The medical profession would seem to better serve its patients by creating procedures that foster the minimal amount of dependence upon itself and its treatments. The knowledge is not yet available for the medical profession to always be successful and therefore it is necessary and only reasonable to make use of whatever options offer hope of recovery. Once recovered, you then have the option to investigate further the underlying causes of your difficulties and change those things in your life that can prevent their recurrence.

I am certain that healing through prayer is a manifestation of Divine intervention and therefore, by definition, is a good thing. I feel that anyone who has received a faith healing as an extension of the miraculous works of God should rightly give credit where credit is due and take a lesson from the experience they have been graced with. To have a personal experience with the forgiving, healing powers of God requires subsequently a reverential change in the person's life.

There are many open questions yet for the researchers. How are people's lives benefited and changed subsequent to recovery at the hands of a faith healing? Is there a greater long-term benefit as a consequence for those who change something in their life style as compared to those who make no changes in their life style? Studies like this would answer questions about the purpose and meaning of healing when it is Divine in origin. Are the consequences different or the same when compared to other mechanism of healing, be they homeopathic or allopathic?

My experiences in the practice of holistic medicine are quite different than those in orthopedics. In the homeopathic experience it appears that the healing process occurs initially or primarily for many conditions with a change in the mental or emotional sphere of the patient. The patient will usually strongly note the physical changes but when questioned will relate that the holistic changes of healing are also happening. As the changes of healing occur at the mental-emotional level, the vital force will then direct the process of change in the physical state of the patient. This results holistically in the patient becoming a healthier version of themselves.

It is harder to go back and reconstruct the sequence of changes in the patient during the development of their disease due to the normal lack of awareness of all the holistic changes occurring. It will take more time and study of long-term results of healing to achieve a complete understanding of the mechanism of healing and the disease process.

Your Healing Heart

Awareness

All Healing is Self-Healing

Law of Similars =
The Healing Law of Nature

Healing = Transforming
Susceptibility into Resistance

Vital Force = "The Big You"

The Disease of Fear

Acceptance

Changing Your Perception of Reality

Being Open-Minded to
Alternative Views of Reality

It's OK to Talk to Yourself
and Listen to Your Body

The Amazing Human Being

Western Medicine has Value
as a Healing System

Forgiveness

The Meaning of Symptoms and Disease

You're OK

Healing: The Never Ending Story
= Learning and Healing Through
Life's Opportunities and Challenges

Chapter 8

The Meaning of Disease

The previous chapters have presented background information to facilitate your understanding of the healing process and the meaning of health. It may help your understanding of the meaning of health to look at its opposite state—that of disease. The disease process has its own set of rules and mechanisms of action. The rules controlling the disease process essentially are the same as the healing process but viewed from the opposite perspective. Both processes ultimately serve the same purpose—your transformation towards holistic health—as a process of going towards a more evolved state of resistance from a previously more vulnerable state of susceptibility.

As you consider this information on the meaning of disease, it helps to frequently remind yourself to keep an open mind. You will be exposed to new concepts that may challenge perceptions that you previously held dear. Being open to a change in your perception of the meaning of any disease that you have could be a strong first step in recovering from that disease. If the disease is a chronic condition, you should at least consider that the current perception you have of the meaning of this disease in your life has not resulted in your recovery. Even if your current perception is supported by all those around you, the possibility of an alternative understanding producing a recovery from your diseases should produce the motivation to considering alternative meanings.

In addition to being open minded, try to take a more holistic view of how the disease process may be manifesting in your life. It is known from centuries of application of the Law of Similars that all symptoms of a disease are part of one energetic healing process. You can complete the healing process by giving yourself more of the same energy as your symptoms. The healing process also occurs holistically, in that all of your symptoms will be relieved at the same time. **Every symptom that is part of your life experience represents a disease process and a healing process.** Knowing and experiencing the reality of this fact can result in a great breakthrough in your understanding the meaning of symptoms.

As you reconsider the meaning of disease in your life, take *all* these facts into account. The Law of Similars is without exception. All symptoms and diseases have a transformative intention for you. Your holistic nature dictates that every symptom is controlled and directed by your vital force. The vital force is capable of integrating all your experiences in life with all of your susceptibilities and resistances. You are always producing the perfect set of symptoms to heal and your current state of health is actually perfect.

If your previous understanding of the meaning of disease was that it was an unfortunate and random blight imposed upon you by some unknown accident of fate—forget that. Your state of health is not a random or illogical occurrence. Life has logic and purpose.

Open yourself to new rules and new understandings. Evaluate life based upon these new principles and then test them out. Discard the unreliable and unscientific. Don't let your judgment be compromised by negative emotions like fear, anger or guilt. Negative emotions can too easily distort your perception. Negativity can limit your ability to evaluate previous assumptions about the meaning of your symptoms. Familiarity can slow your ability to change and grow even when your prior assumptions about the cause of your disease are obviously not correct.

Your susceptibilities and your experiences in life are unique and determine how you will see the world and interpret the events occurring in your life. For this reason, determining the meaning of disease must be done individually. Do not think everyone sees the world the same way you do.

There is a strong tendency to think that your view of the events occurring in life is the correct one. Your perception of the events you witness will only be true for your perspective of life and your prejudices. Your perception of reality and what meaning you give it both determines who you are and is determined by who you are.

To illustrate how your prejudices influence your perspective and view of life, imagine yourself in the following scenario. You are sitting in a large classroom at a nature park with other students waiting for a presentation to begin. The room has windows on most of the walls so you can se the driveway and parking lot that adjoins the building as well as the surrounding gardens.

As everyone is waiting for the lecture to start, you are looking out the window at the gardens. Someone is arriving late for the same presentation and pulls in the driveway in a rush. It is early spring and a young rabbit is crossing the driveway at the wrong time and gets crushed by the car's tire. Most of the people in the class see the rabbit get flattened by the car and watch it squirm for a little while and then go limp. It quickly goes from a cute, little bunny to looking like all the other dead animals you drive by each day on the highway.

Does everybody in the classroom have the same reaction? No. Some student will be sad for the poor rabbit that just got flattened. Other students will be angry because the driver did not slow down to avoid the rabbit; he just rolled right over it and went on his way. Other students don't really take much notice or seem very concerned. The groundskeeper may be happy. He has to clean up the mess, but that is one less rabbit to be digging up and eating those bulbs he planted last fall. You can certainly imagine other possible reactions. You may have a friend who has feelings that are similar to yours, but if you examine their feelings closely you would find differences in the intensity or nature of their reaction.

Let's look at what can be learned from this example. An event occurred—the rabbit got run over by a car. Light waves brought the information of that event into your eyes and the eyes of all the other people in the classroom. It was just an isolated event in life and the same information from that event came to everyone's eyes in the classroom. Each student gave the information of the event their own interpretation, according to who they are. The event became a sad, angry, neutral or happy one, according to their individual nature and life experiences.

Your view of the world and how you interpret the events that you experience is not the same as everyone else's. For the same reason—the fact that you have a unique, individual perception of life—your diseases will be specific to you both in their cause and in the meanings that it holds for you. The meaning your diseases have for you will be related to those transformative experiences necessary for your evolution in life. The nature of this transformative process is the current subject for your study of the healing process.

Hopefully, a new concept of the meaning of diseases will be developing for you. Your diseases represent a call for change in how you perceive the world and the process of healing is the em*bodi*ment of this changing perception. The changing of your perception of the world will occur at the level of your mind. This changed perception will then become manifest in the physical body.

The rabbit story gives you a view of how large is the range of possible interpretations you can have of any and all events that make up your individual experience of life. Your greatest potential state of holistic health will result when you give yourself the freedom to choose any of the possible responses and *do* choose the response that brings you *and* everyone else the greatest joy, peace and ease. The farther you pick from this ideal response choice, the more dis-ease will result for you and all those connected with you.

I would like to offer you another practical example of how your transformed understanding of the meaning of disease is directly linked to how you view the events is your life. Your interpretation of the meaning and the cause of your symptoms will be directly linked to how you have learned to perceive the events you are experiencing. Your health and growth are directly linked to your ability to perceive the true cause or meaning of your symptoms. The presence of any disease as a limitation in your ability to experience a joyful life indicates there must be a limitation or an error in the accuracy of your perception and interpretation of the meaning of the events happening in your life.

I would like to use a common disease for this example. Most people are familiar with the condition known as pneumonia and the fact that the body has a left lung and a right lung. Western physicians are taught in medical school that pneumonia represents an invasion of the body by bacteria or other micro-organisms. The cause of the disease pneumonia is thought to be that you are in a good state of health and you suffer an exposure to and an attack by these organisms. You have to fight off the infection (pneumonia) and bacteria in order to recover good health. This theoretical understanding creates the logic behind the principle of prescribing *anti*biotics, to kill the offending micro-organism.

Western medicine's understanding of the meaning of disease dates back to the germ theory of disease proposed hundreds of years ago by Dr. Pasteur. Dr. Pasteur based his theory upon actual observations he made of changes in the patient's health. He then made interpretations of these observations that were his perception of what these changes meant. Dr. Pasteur observed a marked difference in the condition of their sputum between the healthy patients and the ones with pneumonia. The pneumonia patient produced large amounts of sputum that was abnormal or deranged from the condition of the sputum in a healthy person.

The sputum of the pneumonia patient contained many white blood cells and many bacteria. Dr. Pasteur's interpretation of the altered findings in the pneumonia patient was made possible by the development of the microscope. The microscope allowed greater details about the characteristics of sputum to be directly seen. A common type of bacteria that was found to be associated with the sputum of pneumonia patients even became named pneumococcus. Dr. Pasteur's germ theory appeared to be consistent with the observable facts and has persisted intact to the present time in western medicine.

Where the germ theory may at first glance appear to be consistent with the facts and offer a true explanation of the *cause* of a disease state like pneumonia, a wider view of the observable facts related to pneumonia cast more doubt than verification on the germ theory. The pneumonia example can be a helpful demonstration of the process of being more inclusive in your examination of the facts related to your health. Pneumonia can serve as an example of the process of evaluating your assumptions about reality or truth in the face of a new or enlarged perspective of the phenomenon of disease. This same process is useful in getting a better understanding of the cause or meaning of any of the phenomenon you are exposed to in the world.

In our pneumonia example, remember that anatomically you have a left and a right lung and each lung is divided into several lobes. It is often the case in pneumonia that only one lung or part of one lung is affected with the pneumonia. The unaffected parts of your lungs will remain quite normal to examination with a stethoscope or chest X-ray. Know that your lungs are never sterile. The air we breathe is not sterile. The air you breathe is directed to your lungs through a series of passageways—the mouth, trachea and bronchi. Along this pathway there is no sterilizer, just connecting tubes that have some ability to filter and keep our interior lung surfaces clean, but not sterile. At anytime you could culture the airways for bacteria and find them to be present.

Let's assume our pneumonia patient to have pneumococcal pneumonia of the right lung, as demonstrated by chest X-ray, physical exam and sputum analysis. An interesting fact is that if you would culture the patient's healthy left lung, you would find the pneumococcus bacteria are there—but there is no pneumonia in the left lung. The bacteria occur in smaller numbers in the healthy left lung but they are there

It is possible to make the patient feel better by giving him an antibiotic to kill the pneumococcus. The antibiotics may even appear to speed up the process of recovering health. Interestingly, if you would re-culture the right lung six months after the pneumonia has been recovered and he feels quite well, and all examinations look normal, you will find the pneumococcus again present in the normal culture of bacteria present in the healthy right lung.

When you breathe, the air goes from your mouth down to the lung in about a second. This air is not sterile and does not get sterilized in the second it takes for the air to get into the right lung. Six months later the pneumococcus bacteria and many other organisms can be found in the right lung, but there is no pneumonia. It is equally as likely that if you had cultured the right lung six months before he got pneumonia, you would find the pneumococcus there, and again no pneumonia. These facts are verifiable, reproducible, measurable and predictable—all the requirements of a scientific proof. The germ theory turns out to be a pretty leaky sieve, if being able to hold water represented knowing the true meaning of disease.

There must be a logic that is consistent with all the observable facts in the pneumonia example and help define the meaning and cause of the disease and its symptoms. The more we take a holistic understanding of the cause of disease, the better chance that it will be consistent with all the observable facts. A holistic approach presumes the logic that every part of the body is interconnected and participating equally in producing your ideal state of health at all times. To have a holistic understanding of the complexity of the information being used to determine your state of health, it is helpful to go back to the model of the Big You. The concept of the Big You allows you to understand how your symptoms represent the best adaptation to the circumstances of your life.

In the energetic, holistic model of understanding the meaning of disease, there is the presumption of this dynamic vital force (the Big You) whose capabilities far exceed those of the conscious level of awareness. The vital force is always aware of the state of health of all tissues in the body. In the pneumonia example, the vital force has apparently perceived the situation of the health of the right lung to have accumulated a level of toxicity that is a danger to the health of the body. The holistic, cumulative effects of how our patient has lived his life and the experiences he has had will now have accumulated a level of toxicity in the right lung that has reached a level that requires a healing process to reduce the dangerous level of toxicity. In the energetic understanding of health this toxicity can be physical as well as a mental-emotional experience.

In this holistic model of knowing the meaning of disease, you can understand the Big You as evaluating the condition of your right lung and deciding to take an action to clean itself and reduce the level of toxicity. Your vital force will create the most efficient process possible to do this and will enlist the services of its "friend" the pneumococcus. The vital force is aware of the presence of the pneumococcus in the lungs, because the bacteria have always been there. Through your immune system and the lymph nodes, the vital force monitors all the fluids and tissues of the body. In order to start the healing process, the vital force will create the ideal conditions in the right lung for the proliferation of the pneumococcus. It will change the pH, temperature or some other environmental factor in the lung to create ideal conditions for proliferation of the pneumococcus. The vital force will also direct your immune system's response to the pneumococcus.

Your body is quite well adapted to the environment and makes use of all the available services that bacteria can provide. An adult male will have approximately four pounds of bacteria in his intestinal tract. These bacteria actively participate in the digestive process. You do not do any of the work of digestion that these bacteria are able to do for you. You are quite efficient in making use of anything useful in the environment to save your energy and focus for other things.

Now that the Big You has created this environment of an inflammatory reaction in the lungs, you can observe the cleaning up process in the lung as a process of many things leaving your body in ways or amounts that do not occur in the normal state. You may see large amounts of sputum produced as well as other avenues of detoxification, such as perspiration or diarrhea. The presumed intention of this process in the understanding of energetic, holistic medicine is to get rid of something that is endangering your health.

Western medicine does not consider the possibility that these symptoms or disease process could be purposeful because the focus is on their unpleasant nature. It would be interesting to know what is in these discharges. You might then learn more about the behaviors in your life that are having an adverse effect on your health.

In an energetic system of medicine that works with the body, you can sometime infer the cause of the disease from the remedy that matches your symptoms and accelerates healing. This remedy may be known to be helpful in a specific set of physical or mental-emotional susceptibilities or stresses. When a remedy helps you recover from a disease, it usually means that the time tested association of this remedy with a particular type of stress means that you have a susceptibility to that particular stress.

Killing the bacteria will relieve the symptoms of pneumonia, but that can stop the curative process short of its ideal natural capability. Killing the bacteria may be necessary at times when overwhelming infection can threaten life. This is particularly true when the natural healing efforts of the body have been thwarted in several ways by anti treatments.

Interrupting the natural healing process may lead to the need for more frequent recurrences of the symptoms. This will be particularly true if the underlying cause is not recognized and there is no change in the behaviors that contribute to the toxicity. Being able to discover the meaning of the disease (your susceptibility) and the behaviors that contribute to your need for a symptomatic response will all have the benefit of helping you achieve the best state of health possible. They represent the transformative process that brings you resistance to future occurrences of the disease.

Changing your perception of reality and achieving a new understanding of the meaning of disease is not easy, but has worthwhile consequences. It requires a change that is as basic as how you express your personality. I am optimistic that you have the potential available in your personality to express yourself in a more healthy way and that each of you can achieve more freedom in the interpretation of, and reaction to, the circumstances occurring in your life.

Those components of your personality that need to be recognized for transformation and brought into your awareness are then most efficiently transformed by taking advantage of the healing Law of Similars. The Law of Similars states that if you can identify the susceptibilities in your individual being that are being expressed in a way that needs to be transformed, giving yourself more of that energy automatically takes you in the healing direction. Those qualities of susceptibility that are physical are easier to define than those from the mental-emotional part of your personality.

Homeopathic therapy demonstrates that in chronic or autoimmune diseases, non-physical susceptibilities have greater power in creating your symptoms and ultimately in your healing. The opportunities for healing in working *with* your self and not against it are enormous. It takes some combination of open mindedness, courage, honesty and humility to evaluate your own susceptibilities at the level of your mind. The mind is more elusive and subjective when trying to define the nature of your susceptibilities.

To help illustrate a personal observation that healing occurs holistically in chronic disease, I would like to use another example from my practice. The impression that healing occurs primarily or entirely in the mind and then becomes manifest secondarily in the physical level is just a personal impression or observation. This impression is based on observing people recover their health and what they relate to me as their impression of their experience. Most patients will notice the physical changes most directly but soon notice that other manifestations of health in their life are changing at the same time. I only had the opportunity to notice this when I got out of the rat race of specialty medicine, where the only time I spent more than fifteen minutes with a patient was when they were under general anesthesia.

Peter is a middle-aged man who had been bothered by rheumatoid arthritis for much of his adult life. I had known him for many years as he had needed operations on several of his joints to minimize the sufferings and destruction of his joints. He returned to see me when his symptoms were recurring in the same way as had previously only responded to surgery to get relief. He assumed he would need surgery again.

I had completed my homeopathic training by that time and offered him a homeopathic remedy for his complaint. He was in a lot of pain but agreed to try it for a short while. It did not take very long for his pain to be relieved and he just kept getting better. By about three months his rheumatoid arthritis was nearly all inactive. He still had residual joint deformities from the many years he had his disease, but all the active signs and symptoms were gone.

Peter was quite happy with his recovery and the freedom to enjoy his days with minimal disability. He is a person who naturally has insight into his overall health. He told me that he had noticed that something interesting had changed in his life since taking the homeopathic remedy. In addition to relieving his joint pains, he had noticed an interesting change in himself at work that coincided with the lessening of his pain. He now realized that he had had a problem for a long time at his work with the boss. Things his boss would do or say would get under his skin and make him quite angry and upset. The boss is the boss and he respected that, but it left him with all the force of the anger to affect his health. He was unable to do or say anything that would effect a change or resolve the difficulty at work.

Peter noticed that after taking the remedy, he would go to work and the boss would still be doing the same things that used to make him so upset, but it just didn't anger him anymore. Peter had clearly evolved in his life and was now empowered to choose his reaction to the events in his life. This transformation took him holistically in the direction of his freedom to be healthy and make healthy choices in how he responded to the events in his life. This has become a fairly common observation in my practice of energetic medicine.

Even if patients are focused on their physical complaints, when you ask them to compare the initial symptoms they reported from a personality standpoint to their subsequent evaluation, they will report a very different evaluation of where they are now. Patients are often surprised to recall how strong their former symptoms were and how gradually they moved into a happier state of mind.

An interesting question may then come to your mind: could the patient have gotten to this new healthier version of themselves without having had those initial symptoms plus taking more of the energy of those symptoms? You may answer no if your perception is that the patient had been previously living their life without healing the symptoms and did not seem to be able to elevate themselves above that level of disease. With this understanding, the meaning of their symptoms would appear to be a positive blessing in their life. Their symptoms brought the patient to a place that they had not previously evolved to in life but always had the potential to achieve. It is also possible that some other treatment might be equally curative.

When exploring the concept of the meaning of disease, it may also be helpful to look at the purpose of suffering. There are a couple possibilities of why suffering is a part of disease. If the evolutionary process is to serve the intention of moving you in the direction of better health, suffering could be necessary as the motivating factor to get you moving in that direction. Without suffering, you might just stay as you are (susceptible) and never achieve the ability to control your own health (resistance). You would always remain at the mercy of others and your environment if you never undertook the transformative process that suffering stimulates.

Another possibility is that suffering could be seen to be a self imposed condition that allows you to defer the blame for your condition in life to some outside factor. It does seem that those people who see themselves as victims of some external factor remain in the state of chronic disease for a long time. People who tend to be self empowered or were previously victims who become self-empowered seem to be able to move out of suffering and minimize its impact on their lives.

Both the decisions you make in life or how you react to events in your life seem to have the potential to determine whether these event will become an isolated acute one or will develop into a chronic disease. Seeing events as a challenge to overcome will tend to keep it as an acute event in your life. If you feel weak or overwhelmed by the events in your life, you will have a tendency to become a chronic sufferer.

It is actually not uncommon in orthopedic surgery to see people who are injured even decide at a conscious or subconscious level to maximize their suffering in order to maximize the benefits that can come to them following an injury. It is called "the greenback syndrome" in the orthopedic literature and is actively promoted by the legal profession that stands to also gain a percentage of the profit from suffering. Suffering is therefore able to serve a number of different purposes as one component of understanding the meaning a disease may have in your life.

Either the experience of practicing homeopathic medicine or your experience in taking homeopathic remedies can offer some insight into the purpose of symptoms and the meaning of disease. When beginning a patient on a moderate potency of a homeopathic remedy, you will often give them one dose and wait.

After taking the correctly chosen remedy, the patient will have a decrease in the intensity of their symptoms for a period of time and then have no further improvement. If you continue to wait, the intensity of the symptoms may start to return to where it was originally. Once you see the symptoms returning, you repeat the remedy and should expect to see a second period of improvement that lasts about the same time interval as the first. When you learn the time interval that the remedy can act, you can shorten the time interval at which you give the remedy and the patient will experience a steady improvement in their symptoms.

Several insights can be gained by observing the homeopathic healing process. These observations can have a significant bearing on your understanding of the purpose of symptoms and the meaning of your diseases. The most important observation is that your body demonstrates the variable potential to either heal the symptoms or to produce more of the symptoms. Since one dose of the remedy may act to start a healing process that lasts for weeks, it is clear that you are doing the healing in response to the information that the remedy represents. Whether the body produces more symptoms or a healing of the symptoms can be reproducibly turned from one to the other with the use of the remedy.

While taking a homeopathic remedy, certain events can cause your symptoms to be increased or to reappear. As you observe yourself needing to repeat the remedy to control symptoms, a pattern will develop. You can differentiate those things that you have the freedom to respond to in a healthy way ad not increase symptoms from those things where your freedom to respond is limited and they will produce symptoms. With further repetitions of the remedy you will gain more power over those events that previously caused you to respond by producing symptoms.

This observation allows you to gain insight into your particular susceptibilities and the decisions you are making of how to respond to them. This insight has the potential to show you the road map for your transformation. The transformative purpose of your symptoms becomes quite clear. If you do not recognize this need and its potential, this disease will not be able to demonstrate its meaning for you, and the symptoms will become chronic. If and when you profit from your symptoms and understand the meaning they offer you in life, you can recover good health and a state of ease in life.

As you recover a state of good health, these prior symptoms will not be present anymore. They have served their purpose in your evolution and you now have resistance to these diseases. This disease has been added to the long list of other diseases that you have never had or will ever have because you have full resistance to them. Whatever holistic meaning they represent, you already have a full grasp of it.

To see symptoms and diseases as only your undeserved sufferings in life is clearly a misperception. Unfortunately, this misperception will tend to make them necessary and chronic. Your symptoms can actually contribute to a more holistic appreciation of your potential for good health and achieving full enjoyment from life.

Understanding the helpful purpose of your symptoms can become complementary to all your more obvious qualities you recognize as positive. If you continue to ignore the potential benefits that symptoms offer, you will shut yourself off from knowing the truth of your highest potential expression. The science of homotoxicology indicates that as you ignore your evolutionary stimulus, not only do the symptoms become chronic; there is a progression towards experiencing even more serious diseases.

Healing has been often referred to in this book as either a potentiality or a reality based upon whether you work against or with your symptoms. Healing has already been demonstrated as a possibility by many others and they are all your equal. You can heal most things, or at a minimum, not suffer needlessly from your experience of life. Suffering can end when its purpose in your life is understood to be meant for your evolution and accepted for exactly that and nothing else. You have the power to heal but only manifest it when you make the choices that lead in the direction of healing.

When your symptoms continue to persist, it means you have made the choice not to change and to not evaluate the meaning of your symptoms and their cause. You have chosen to let external circumstances overpower you. Many factors can contribute to making the decision to allow symptoms to continue (fear, guilt, and lack of self confidence) but only you give them their power. The decisive factors in the decision are all inside you, not outside factors.

There are three levels of evolution in your thought and healing process that symbolize the stages necessary to achieve a successful recovery of optimal health and enjoyment in your life. They are *awareness—acceptance—forgiveness.* The first step is **awareness.** All the healing principles that are being proposed to you in this book are about you becoming aware of who you are and the processes you are using to create either your state of health or disease.

Acceptance is the second necessary requirement for self-empowered healing. You need to accept that you have the power to heal yourself and can utilize many available processes and circumstances to further your healing. Acceptance includes the understanding that all the circumstances in your life are providing you opportunities to heal and evolve. Other people are always providing opportunities for you to experience your reactions to them and evaluate your response. Acceptance can develop a healthy response to life that benefits you and everyone else. In the holographic phenomenon of life, you are also participating in everyone else's life around you for their growth and strengthening as well.

The full implication of combining awareness and acceptance together brings you to the point of knowing **forgiveness.** Forgive yourself for the steps and missteps along the way to finding your transformative path. Forgive all others for their participation in your process of growth. You needed their stimulus to find your own susceptibilities and overcome them. Similarly, the others around you need your input in their own process of transformation. They have an equal need for acceptance and awareness to reach this same level of forgiveness for themselves and all others. This interplay of people and energies in our world can have a net positive evolutionary result. Being aware of this fact and the steps of the process will benefit everyone in finding their path and moving along it in a positive direction.

Your Healing Heart

Awareness

All Healing is Self-Healing

Law of Similars =
The Healing Law of Nature

Healing = Transforming
Susceptibility into Resistance

Vital Force = "The Big You"

The Disease of Fear

Acceptance

Changing Your Perception of Reality

Being Open-Minded to
Alternative Views of Reality

It's OK to Talk to Yourself
and Listen to Your Body

The Amazing Human Being

Western Medicine has Value
as a Healing System

Forgiveness

The Meaning of Symptoms and Disease

You're OK

Healing: The Never Ending Story
= Learning and Healing Through
Life's Opportunities and Challenges

Chapter 9

You're OK

The intention of this chapter is to extend the concept that all symptoms are good things. This thought presents an interesting challenge for you: is there a concept similar to the meaning of your symptoms that can be applied to all aspects of your health? Is there any evidence to support a wider understanding of the meaning of your health in relation to the experiences occurring in your life? Is there an overall, discernable plan that is fulfilling a transformative or evolutionary overall purpose in your life? There may be some evidence to support that this is the case. The evidence may be less certain than the Law of Similars but it has an overall direction that gives some validity to speculation about the intention of why events occur when they do.

This chapter will necessarily include softer data or intuitive impressions than the more rigid scientific rules of homeopathic medicine. Since there will always be some uncertainty in answering questions like what is the purpose of disease or what is the meaning of life, it is necessary to grant leeway to accommodate individual interpretations of the meaning of the experiences you have in life. You need to be flexible enough to change your interpretation of the meaning of the events in your life when your current understanding does not explain new facts.

An interesting example of the need for flexibility in interpreting new facts when you encounter them in life could be provided by studying astrology. Astrology is not something that would seem to merit serious consideration to an investigator who preferred to take a reasoned, scientific approach in understanding the meaning contained in the occurrence of events in your life. Though scientific reasoning trains you to be open to all possibilities and then design experiments to test a new theory. The results from testing the interaction between a variety of different influences will prove or disprove the predictability or reliability of the theory. Who does the experiment, when it is done and where it is done should not be factors in predicting the outcome. The result that is obtained will be scientifically valid when determined only by the application of the natural laws of science to the variables being tested. The science of astrology does not appear initially to have any relationship to medical science.

My personal impression of astrology was that it was not relevant to how I lived my life. Surgeons by nature have a captain-of-the-ship mentality. Surgeons make important decisions in people's lives and direct the details of carrying them out according to well defined principles. I certainly felt in charge when I made decisions in my life and that these decisions were made according to my own training and my best intentions for all involved.

When all is said and done, the surgeon takes both the credit and the responsibility for his actions and their consequences. I did not consider that someone or something else had any hand in the decisions that were made when I was presented with a choice in surgery or life. Sources from outside of myself would have an influence in providing information used to make decisions, but ultimately it was my decision. Life appears to contain a balance between presenting you with a range of possibilities for your decision making and a variety of results that will follow your decisions. Your free will enables you to make individual choices from among all the possibilities.

It is from this perspective that several years ago on Father's Day, one of my daughters gave me the "present" of an appointment with an astrologer. Neither one of us had any prior experiences with astrologers, but thought it would be a fun thing to do. We scheduled appointments for the weekend and gave the astrologer only our first names, birth cities and birth dates to the minute. She knew nothing else about us. The price of the reading was not enough that anyone could afford to invest time in researching who we are. I have a pretty good poker face and felt I would be able to not signal her into giving answers that she might try to read from my body language. I even had a plan to lead her astray into inaccurate information, if I sensed we had encountered some phony charlatan.

From the moment I sat down, the astrologer began telling me who I was while thumbing through astrological charts that gave her this information. She asked hardly any questions and I did not need to reveal any information to her. She did not know what my profession was, but otherwise nailed down exactly the characteristics of my personality and many previous and current events that were occurring in my life. It was an unsettling experience, in that a total stranger could predict the events in my life, and my natural responses to them, from the orientation of the starts in the sky when I was born.

My daughter followed and her experience was exactly the same. I can say that my initial reaction was one of amazement and resistance. I still like the thought that I am in charge of my life and didn't particularly like thinking there was some cosmic play going on that I had a predetermined role in. She made a number of predictions for the next year that were surprisingly accurate. Like the fact that on September 18 my son would get his first job after college. Sure enough that was the day he was hired as a pharmaceutical rep. Other predictions the astrologer made did not come to pass. My subsequent experiences with astrology lead me to have a partial acceptance of the concept of predeterminism or astrology. The accuracy of the information from astrologers varies according to their skill level. It would seem that life contain a balance between presenting you with prescribed possibilities for you to experience, but you maintain your individual ability to make choices from among the possibilities.

You have the freedom to act as you choose, but there may be a more universal plan than the individual plan you make. This plan of the stars or universe has a hand in determining the choices you are going to get to make. It is from this only slightly clear perspective that I urge you to give consideration to any of the rules that can be discovered about this cosmic plan that brings you the opportunities for your symptoms and your healing. Most specifically, it would be helpful to know how this plan may pertain to your present and future state of health.

If an intelligent force could establish the universe with its laws like gravity and the Law of Similars, there may be another plan that it is appropriate to research. Studying the principles of this plan may help you move more efficiently along the path that leads to greater ease or health. The point is **not** to use astrological predictions to determine your actions. *The point is to be more open minded in considering what might be the nature of the underlying forces at work in presenting you with your symptoms and diseases in life!*

In considering your potential for having either good health or disease, the following speculations are presented from an optimistic standpoint that you're ok. You exist in a world where both benevolence and danger always exist together as possibilities. The presumption is being made that it is far better to look for the good in life and to initially expect to find it. Having optimism needs to be a realistic possibility or it will become counter productive to improving your overall health.

In order to discover the underlying principles determining your state of health, you will want to take an expanded view of the evidence. Search for the meaning that can be inferred from the events occurring in your life and how your reaction to them brings about changes in your health. *The better you understand the rules and principles at work in determining your health, the less friction you will experience on your path thru life.* You will have an easier time maintaining good health or achieving better health, if you understand how your health challenges can be turned into opportunities for healing.

It is easy to get caught up in day to day details of living life and miss the significance of something that has a strong impact on your health. You need to take a more holistic look at your health, as being equally dependent upon your mental-emotional state as your physical state. Physical symptoms can be more visibly apparent and be painful in a very concrete way, but should not eliminate your awareness of the impact that suffering at the mental-emotional level can have on your overall enjoyment of life.

In trying to appreciate a holistic view of all the factors that might be going into determining your present and future state of health, it will be instructive to go back and examine yourself as the amazing human being. Recall that your conscious awareness is only a small part of who you are (the little you). The ability of your conscious mind to determine your state of health is enormously dwarfed by the capability of the whole you that includes the Big You. The conscious mind's awareness of all the factors that are contributing to producing your state of health, at any moment, is only a tiny fraction of the massive amount of information actually being used to continually perfect your health.

Is what you are able to observe of your amazing ability to heal, (your ability to constantly produce your ideal state of health and to provide yourself information in the way of symptoms to remove susceptibilities), all that is possible? How complete is your conscious awareness of all the factors you might be making use of to produce these amazing results? Since your potential for healing and transforming yourself has a net positive effect on your enjoyment of life, optimism about the purpose of life and disease would seem to have a rational basis. Death and disease are certainly realities, but looking at the whole perspective of life from birth to death will be your framework for judging its net effect.

If the overall intended purpose of life was negative it would seem more likely that you would start life at birth with your best state of health and deteriorate from there. You actually have your greatest number of susceptibilities at birth. Through the benefit of life experiences, you progressively transform these susceptibilities into resistances. You will naturally experience ups and downs in life as you are actively participating in the transformative process of individual evolution. The general trend is in the direction of strengthening and resistance.

Keep a holistic framework in mind for this evolutionary process. During life you will develop a physical type of resistance that can be measured immunologically. This transformative process is quite active in youth and middle age. You will also experience a mental-emotional transformation as a result of your life experiences and these changes are more characteristic of the growth accumulated in middle and older age.

The emphasis has previously been upon individualization of patients and staying away from lumping them together into diagnostic categories to then apply a standard of care treatment. It may seem contradictory to now be emphasizing a holistic approach towards understanding the meaning of your state of health and generalizing this principle to large groups of people. The emphasis has been on *discovering universal principles of healing* and health that could be applied to each individual. *Now you will be asked to consider if these principles have correlations throughout your whole life that help to explain the appearance of diseases at various times in your life as well as in the life of others.*

Some diseases such as infections are epidemic and therefore your individual susceptibility must be shared with others. In the case of an epidemic, you might be sharing a susceptibility to the influence of a particular virus. When the virus enters the population, the presence of a shared susceptibility by a large number of people in a group makes the epidemic first a possibility and then a reality. Due to the holistic nature of your expression of symptoms, the population may also share susceptibilities at the mental or emotional layer. It might be possible in the case of a collapse of the stock market that many people are sharing a susceptibility to fear of the future and they react similarly to bad news by selling stocks more than they are buying stocks.

The answer to these types of questions will be determined by considering the types of influences that may affect your behavior and secondarily your health. How susceptible or resistant you might be as an individual or a member of a group to things like viruses, thoughts, the weather or your feelings have been considered as important determinants of your health for 3000 years in the Chinese system of medicine. All these factors are considered as energies that determine the health of individuals and groups of people. This is not yet a common source of understanding or study in western medicine.

The next goal for your study of health is to *understand the balance between how much the decisions you make are influenced by your conscious interpretation of the events in your life and your extra-conscious interpretation.* You are aware of your conscious mind's interpretation of the significance of the factors you consider in making your choices in life. You have conscious awareness of the external events and your internal attitudes that influence the choices you make. Your response to these factors will have an influence on your state of health. Your extra-conscious awareness greatly exceeds the capabilities of our conscious awareness but both have important roles in determining your health.

In seeking to understand why you have the symptoms that you do, the emphasis will still be on taking personal responsibility for your health and actions. Seeing yourself as a victim of external factors is short-sighted and not conducive to healing. The needed change in perspective is to have a more holistic appreciation of all the influences on you to understand your response to them. The shift in emphasis is to look at your response and the response of others around you to the same influences. You need to realize that you are sharing influences from many factors on your health with others. You will have some unique responses to these influences and some similar responses.

If everyone moved in lock step to the influences of the world, there would be strong, sudden shifts in behaviors and health. This type of reaction would cause chaos. Our individual differences maintain a more gradual evolution in the direction of greater resistance. Keep this balance between your individual response and group responses in mind in your attempt to discover the influence that events have on your own state of health.

It may be helpful to revisit the difference between curative and palliative therapies. The difference between the results of these two types of therapy can facilitate an examination of the meaning of your health and the philosophy that says you're ok in where your health is and where it is going. Defining available treatments as either curative or palliative will be easier to understand if they are first looked at in relation to individuals and later consider its application to groups.

The most reliable way to know if a treatment that you have chosen or have received is going to have a palliative or curative effect on the body is to just wait for while and observe. Your body will invariably give you the answer. All you have to do is be aware that you are getting the answer, when it comes. It may not always be directly obvious to you.

For the purpose of this analysis, the general definition of a palliative treatment will be one that is able to remove the symptoms for which it was recommended but does not have an effect on the underlying susceptibility. Your susceptibility to the initiating cause that was the reason for your production of the symptoms will remain unchanged. *It will help you identify a treatment as palliative when you see any of the following events occur in your health after a palliative treatment has been received.* You may develop a side effect from the treatment. The original symptoms may recur again after the treatment is stopped. There will not be a noticeable improvement in your overall signs of good health.

In contrast, a treatment that is curative will not produce side effects and recurrences of the original condition should be less severe and less frequent than previously. This increased level of resistance should be accompanied by an overall improvement in your signs of good health.

The patient's response to treatment will demonstrate what type of treatment has been chosen for them. Putting together a timeline of their health history can be useful in understanding the relationship between different diseases in a person's life. Diseases may have occurred at different times in life but represent the same susceptibility. Women who have had a hysterectomy are a good example of the difference between choosing a palliative or a curative treatment.

During my surgical training and practice it was a common feeling among the medical practitioners that if a woman had completed having the family she desired and was troubled by uterine symptoms of pain or bleeding, the best answer was hysterectomy. The uterus was considered somewhat of a throwaway organ in this situation. There was thought to be no real downside to its absence. Hysterectomies are common in surgical suites and given little attention as long as there are some symptoms or the findings of a fibroid.

Practicing holistic medicine gives an entirely different appraisal of hysterectomy as a clearly palliative form of treatment for symptoms of uterine pain or bleeding. It would at first glance appear to be an entirely curative treatment if your focus is only that of a surgical specialist. When you take the whole patient into account and look at a longer time frame in their life, the hysterectomy is probably not curative but only palliative.

In homeopathic medicine a complete timeline of the patient's symptoms and the sequence of appearance of all symptoms in a person's life are considered to be significant expressions of healing. The practitioner is always looking for a single remedy that would be indicated by all the symptoms that have appeared at various times in the patient's life. This remedy will be the most powerfully curative remedy that can be offered to that patient. The goal of finding a life-long pattern of expressing one energy state in multiple organ systems of the body will tie the patient's health history together in a logical continuum.

Treating according to this continuum of susceptibility offers them the best chance for making marked gains in their health.

Having the opportunity to search for these patterns over and over again in patients will help demonstrate certain principles of healing. These principles will determine your ability to find a treatment for today that you can presuppose will prevent a future progression of symptoms. If the underlying cause or susceptibility can be treated, there is a good chance the body will no longer need to produce further symptoms. The vital force will have achieved its goal of profiting from experiences in this area of susceptibility, and can attain a state of enhanced resistance. This state of enhanced resistance should prevent future occurrences of a similar disease unless the strength of the challenging event becomes overwhelmingly strong.

This principle of more than one disease state representing one underlying susceptibility is often seen in the case of women who have had hysterectomies. It almost always seems to be the case that within six to twelve months of having the hysterectomy, the patient will have the onset in their life of a whole new set of symptoms or disease complex.

It seems that the uterine symptoms of cramping or hemorrhage are the body's symptomatic response to a particular susceptibility having been encountered in the patient's life. The uterine symptoms represent a counter balancing action of the body that was purposeful in the overall process of healing. For some reason, the uterine symptoms were chosen as the healing response to the stress that occurred in the patient's area of susceptibility.

When the organ of expression was removed from the body, the symptoms were dealt with, but the underlying cause was not addressed. The Big You is quite aware of this situation and will then select the next best outlet for expression to continue or reawaken the intent of the process—healing or transformation to resistance. The variety of new disease expressions can include many of the other organ systems of the body. It is common to see in practice, new diseases that would fall into the category of auto-immune disorders. You might typically see a new disease appear like rheumatoid arthritis or severe migraines.

Because the appearance of the secondary disease is not usually in days to weeks, but is in terms of months, the pattern is usually not apparent unless you go looking for it. The common link between the two disease states only becomes apparent when the most effective homeopathic remedy for their second disease also covers as well the previous symptoms from the uterus. It may also be the case that the same remedy will cover well the symptoms of a disease that occurred prior to the onset of uterine symptoms. A condition like chronic allergies or hypertension may have been the symptoms that were suppressed initially, and this incited the need for the balancing expression of hemorrhage from the uterus.

In a curative approach to the treatment of uterine dysfunction, the treatment should recover normal function and structure of the uterus, appropriate for the age of the patient. When an ideal match can be found for the symptoms with a homeopathic remedy, not only will the patient be relieved of their symptoms, but they may experience better energy, emotional balance, more restful sleep and other signs of good health. If the remedy matches symptoms that are occurring in other organ systems of the body, they will be relieved as well.

Particularly in the case where the uterine symptoms represent a malignancy, it is important to find the underlying cause for the occurrence of the disease and treat it. Otherwise, removing the uterus will leave the need for expression intact in the body. This expression may later be found in other parts of the body as metastasis. It is hard to understand the meaning of distant spread of a localized disease in the body without a different or broader concept of the purpose of a malignant disease process.

Is it possible to understand the logic of how or why a malignant disease—or any disease that is potentially fatal—can be serving a purpose in a holistic understanding of health? This is again an area where your conscious mind is too limited in its understanding of all the influences impacting your state of health.

There may be solid logic in the possibility that when the amount of joy in your life is greatly overwhelmed by the amount of suffering in your life, the rational action would be to end your life. In considering the balance of joy or suffering in a person's life, all influences must be considered—physical, mental and emotional—cumulatively over your life. This is the view your vital force has available in determining your state of health.

An important factor in this equation would have to be the history of success or lack of success with your attempts to overcome the suffering. At your most expanded level of awareness, you can see the history of your attempts to overcome your susceptibilities and make a measurement of the likelihood of future success based on past experiences. When a patient is overwhelmed by a mental-emotional state of sadness, grief, despair, guilt, fear or hopelessness; it may lead to cancer as a socially acceptable form of ending the suffering.

Studying the patients who experienced long term recoveries from terminal cancer documented in "Remarkable Recoveries" may give some validity to this hypothesis. The homeopathic treatment of cancer has a high degree of success documented over 200 years through the application of the Law of Similars. The subtle energy of a homeopathic remedy seems to have the ability to affect people at a level that can bring about a remission of the disease process of cancer.

The high dilution potencies used in the treatment of cancer likely have a primary action of affecting the mental emotional aspect of the patient strongly. To effect a holistic change in a person at the level of their thoughts and feelings and then observe a recovery of the physical can be a quite instructive process to observe. Many cases have been documented of recovery of serious disease following a change in attitude. The change may be the recovery of a feeling of joy or laughter into the patient's life or something quite concrete like changing your job.

It is a little strange and challenging to conventional wisdom to say you're ok when you have cancer. Could it be reasonable to say you're ok with cancer? Possibly so, if the balance of influences in your life is overwhelmingly negative and without a reasonable hope of recovery. It would then be appropriate for your treatment to make an assessment of this balance and come up with a plan that deals with the basic cause of the unfavorable balance. Only at this level might you affect a significant change in the balance that can trigger the self-healing process. This is consistent with the concept that your current health is a consequence of all the prior events in your life combined with the natural balance of strengths and weaknesses that you came into life with.

You can also see what initially appear to be self-destructive behaviors in patients that have some similarity in appearance to the self-destructive nature of tumors and auto-immune diseases. It seems paradoxical that patients will persist in behaviors that are clearly known to be contrary to maintaining good health. Due to the harmful nature of these behaviors, their detrimental effects are usually well publicized and generally known to the patient. Ignorance or being unaware are not plausible excuses. The best examples of these persistent harmful behaviors are seen in the area of addictive behaviors. Patients often will persist in the use of a wide variety of harmful substances even when they have already started to demonstrate their harmful effects in symptoms. These substances can include a long list of common "vices" in our present day world—alcohol, overeating, cigarettes, sugar, coffee, marijuana or narcotics.

It seems almost unbelievable in orthopedic practice to have diabetic patients who have already lost one leg to gangrene continue to smoke and sneak sweets into their diet. They willingly put their remaining limb in peril. It was often astounding to see how poor the care these patients might give to the condition of their remaining foot when they know the consequences can be severe. The combination of lack of recognition of the danger and disregard for their welfare is puzzling. The puzzle again likely represents having a limited understanding of all the cumulative influences on this individual's life that make this a logical behavior.

If this presumption is true [*all symptoms and states of health are created perfectly as a response to each patient's experiences in life and their unique nature as a set of susceptibilities*]; there must be logic to self destructive and addictive behaviors. The use of harmful substances such as alcohol, tobacco or drugs must be understood to be purposeful actions of the patient to self-medicate themselves to balance some level of discomfort. This discomfort is likely not recognized or easily available for correction at the conscious level. These behaviors represent a transformative, healing process that is controlled outside of their conscious awareness.

Your holistic awareness is capable of sensing the imbalances that have been created in your health and a need for corrective action to rebalance your health. Curative treatments require a mechanism to achieve balance in both the short and long term. Substances that satisfy a craving provide a short term rebalancing but are not contributing to the long term restoration of better health. The pleasure principle of avoiding pain seems to overwhelm the longer term goal of achieving resistance through transformation.

Smoking and the use of illegal drugs would both clearly be destructive behaviors that are contrary to long term of survival and maintaining good health. The strong association between smoking and cancer may be logical in the holistic sense. Smoking may provide relief, in the present moment, from the suffering associated holistically with a stress or strain in life. Smoking will not provide long-term relief from the cause of the suffering. Healing requires a compelling reason to prolong life. This will not be the case if life means ongoing suffering.

In Chinese medicine, the lung meridian and the physical lung are known to be the area in the body that is susceptible to and stores the emotions of grief, sorrow or sadness. These are not influences that are considered in western medicine in the evaluation of the cause of tobacco addiction and its treatment. This less than holistic approach to evaluation and therapy may be an underlying reason why the treatment of addictive disorders has not proven to be very successful in the long term.

A more successful approach to the treatment of persistent, addictive or destructive behaviors that have detrimental consequences on your health would be to start with a holistic understanding that you're ok. Your behaviors are logical and functional adaptations you are making to the circumstances of your life. Attempting to enforce restrictive or punitive therapies will only add to the cumulative negative influences in the person's life. Punitive therapies will likely be self perpetuating of both the need for therapy and the persistence of the underlying behaviors. It may paradoxically support the therapy more than the patient.

It must be admitted that most punitive treatment programs that do not deal with the need the substance provides can only have short term success. If an addictive behavior is strongly suppressed, it will likely be replaced by another. This can be observed to be a common result of suppressive types of therapy. If you go to an Alcoholics Anonymous meting, you will likely notice the presence of another medication having been substituted for alcohol; often cigarettes or coffee. Similarly, most dieters find themselves yo-yoing up and down with an overall increase in their weight over the years following a short-term success. It is an over-riding principle that you will seek to escape discomfort and the mental emotional discomforts may be a stronger motivating factor then the physical ones. It the treatment adds discomfort such as deprivation or frustration, it will add to the need for a balancing comfort.

Therapies that start from the approach that you're ok and understand you are doing the right thing will seek out the cause of the destructive behaviors. The treatment prescribed will then attempt to find a correction at the causative level. For many of the reasons already discussed this requires a level of understanding that will not be easily ascertained in a few minutes or by looking at only one location or function of the body. Evaluation and treatment needs to be holistic to have a good chance of being permanently curative.

It is easy to see the power of holistic influences on health when looking at cases where this awareness is given no consideration and the cause of the disease remains undiscovered. The cause can be especially elusive when it is at the mental-emotional level. Patients and physicians are not as well trained to look at this level and see what is there. It is an especially strong demonstration of this fact when patients will stop returning for their appointments when the treatment benefits them and they are recovering from their disease. This unfortunate reality of un-holistic therapy was demonstrated to me early in my training in acupuncture.

The instructor had a patient with amyotrophic lateral sclerosis (ALS) that demonstrated this principle well. The patient was a middle aged man whose family brought him in for treatment with electro-acupuncture for his ALS. ALS is a severe, progressive disease where the average time from diagnosis to death is only three years. The patient's wife brought him for treatments, as he was not very interested or receptive to electro-acupuncture. Despite his reluctance to return for treatment, she brought him in every month for nine years and the disease was slightly improved and he never progressed in his disability. After nine years of successful treatment, the patient moved out of state and never returned for any treatments. His disease reactivated and he was dead in less than three years. The patient had always resisted his treatments and they were only done due to the influence of his wife. The patient actually wanted to leave the area and stop his treatments.

This treatment was obviously strictly palliative and did not reach the curative level by treating the underlying purpose his disease was serving for him. It is a frequent observation that patients who are brought in reluctantly by the family will not be as compliant or do as well with their treatments. Your relationships with others around you and their support can be a positive or a negative influence on your recovery of health. The primary decision to heal or not is made by you at a level that has its most powerful influence outside of your conscious awareness.

I have found the change to a homeopathic practice to be most rewarding in treating patients with cancer and autoimmune diseases. The therapeutic power of holistic or homeopathic medicine to achieve a lasting recovery and resistance to recurrence of disease can take you beyond the initial removal of symptoms accomplished by the application of the Law of Similars. This lasting transformative process that curative healing represents is enhanced by taking a lengthy and complete history of all the symptoms throughout your life. *The homeopathic remedies initially act according to the Law of Similars, but the treatments become deeply curative when your conscious awareness of what the symptoms represent is enhanced.* This is the main reason I have written this book for my patients and anyone else who chooses to study the healing process. All symptoms are examined as to when they occurred in your life and what changes or events occurred in your life prior to the onset of each symptom.

In the homeopathic history, a search is made for a pattern of recurring new symptoms and similar types of stress that preceded their appearance. It is helpful for you to understand that the purpose of collecting all this information is to find your susceptibilities as the underlying cause for the reactive symptoms your body is producing.

The homeopathic physician is trying to find a logical sequence to your symptoms. The goal is to become aware of what the symptoms represent as your reaction to an underlying susceptibility having been encountered. Your recovery will be more permanent if in the process you are also able to recognize the meaning of your symptoms and the pattern of their occurrence over the entire span of your life. This awareness will help strengthen you in a way that decreases the likelihood you will react to the same stress in the future with similar symptoms.

It helps your healing to reinforce the concept that all symptoms represent a healing process. Attaching negative emotions to your symptoms is inappropriate and not helpful to recovery. It helps healing more to be aware of the appropriateness of your symptoms. The symptoms need to be recognized for the potential benefits they represent in the transformation process of removing susceptibilities. This awareness can tip the balance of health in the recovery direction and away from disease. If you can reduce the power of negative emotions like despair, blame and guilt it will be important in changing the direction that your health is taking.

I am obviously trying to create for you an optimistic world view and an appreciation of the fact you're ok. It is then reasonable to have some hope of relief no matter what state of health you find yourself with. It challenges an optimistic view of the world and the concept that ultimately you're ok to see so much suffering and disease in the world. Either these concepts are incorrect or the meaning and purpose of all the suffering you see is beyond a superficial assessment of the purpose it may be serving.

To find insight into the higher order of perspective beyond the information your five senses bring your conscious awareness, it is helpful to revisit the phenomenon of faith healing. There is currently a popular following for a group composed of a catholic priest, a nun and a physician who are doing faith healing sessions for large numbers of people in northern Ohio. They have produced many well publicized cases of spontaneous recovery of people from their complaints. The number of people reporting "healing" cannot be dismissed as a hoax.

If a healing force has the ability to intercede in this world and remove suffering and disease, the next question would then be why in these certain cases and not all those other people who are suffering and praying for relief? If it is true that you're ok, even in your suffering state, what has occurred in those people who are healed by a means outside themselves? What makes them different than they were before being healed? Is the means of healing truly outside of themselves? Is it entirely outside of themselves or only partially?

These questions bear directly on the purpose of suffering and the purpose of healing. As part of the insight process involved in understanding a holistic transformation of your health, you must look for the purpose that negative influences on your health are serving. The power to heal behind this insight might be in the awareness that you're ok. *Your ability to forgive those who are participating in the process of bringing you the stresses to initiate the process of healing is as important as forgiving yourself for all your symptoms.* Removing the weight of all this negativity gives power to the healing process.

The faith healer may be taking a short cut approach to this level of awareness when the person healed feels that he has been chosen to be forgiven or absolved of the consequences of the negative influences in his life. This explanation is theoretical, but consistent with the underlying process of your healing as getting to a level of awareness that you're ok now, or soon will become ok as you release negativity and recover your best health. Having a close encounter with the power of the divine could be a fast track to awareness that the world is ultimately controlled by a force for good and that absolution and resolution of symptoms are possible. *The overall purpose of this study is for you to realize that healing through awareness and forgiveness is within your capabilities as demonstrated by others and is equally contained within everyone.*

The highlight of this process is to be aware of the reason for your suffering and accept this as a necessary step in a strengthening process. This is not about being a martyr. Learn your life lessons and move on to health. Free yourself from blame or guilt by any means that either removes the obstacles to healing or puts into place the mechanisms for healing to start. Keep in mind the rules you have learned to recognize a truly curative process. Then you should not have to repeat the symptom lesson. Feeling aligned to a higher power may facilitate this transition.

Before leaving the concept of you're ok, it may be worthwhile to speculate further on the question of whether disease is playing a role only in your life as a solitary individual. This question is about defining the outer boundary of the sphere of who you are at the level that has been designated as the Big You. The Big You is an illusive, energetic manifestation of your total awareness. The Big You is receptive to subtle energies coming from great distances. This can be experienced when you think about someone and they will think of you at the same time. They may call or write or just think about you without contacting you, but some communication and interaction has occurred at a subtle energy level that easily spans long distances.

The interaction of people at the subtle energy level is difficult to examine or quantify. Understanding these interactions may be helpful in deciphering the meaning of your symptoms. The question is whether there is some other level of communication influencing your health. Other people certainly have a physical role in creating the situations that occur in your life. Non-physical influences are probably playing a role also.

Knowing how these types of communication influence your health would help you profit from the experiences that ultimately need to be overcome as one of your susceptibilities. Your symptoms or your actions may be providing a stress necessary for someone else to heal. The other person may need the input of your symptoms in their life to be able to gain a particularly valuable insight in their evolution. It is difficult to know if we are interconnected, in this way, at the level of our most subtle energetic manifestations. The philosophical or theological literature suggests that this is a true part of the reality of our state of existence, but it is hard for medical science to document that we are all one at some level.

Epidemic diseases are probably the best area to study the energetic interaction of groups of people. It might be possible to determine if those members of a society that are susceptible to an infectious agent share some more holistic characteristic at the susceptibility level. Flu season is associated with the late winter season. Is there a factor besides the influence of weather that makes some people susceptible to the flu at this time of the year and others not susceptible?

During the flu season everyone experiences the same changes in the weather. People will have individual levels of vitality and different levels of stress occurring in their life. It would be interesting to see if years with high stresses such as loss of financial insecurity, lack of adequate food or an increasing threat of war have more cases of the flu. A study of individual cases would not help, but it should be possible to look for statistical trends in large populations.

Taking an epidemiologic and sociological look at the incidence of diseases like polio following World War II or the Spanish Flu after World War I could be instructive in that millions of people were involved in the diseases.

Homeopathic medicine offers some insight into the possibility that other factors might be acting to determine the occurrence of epidemic diseases. Homeopathy also offers a possible mechanism to further investigate the causes of epidemics.

Historically, when an epidemic disease occurs, the large majority of patients will experience the disease in varying severities but all the patients will have similar symptoms. For this reason, once several patients have been found to recover with one homeopathic remedy, that same remedy can be used to treat the large majority of patients suffering from the same epidemic. This is because the remedy matches the common symptoms found in all of the patients.

Since one homeopathic remedy can treat the majority of patients in an epidemic, it can be presumed that they all have the same susceptibility. The specific virus or bacteria that caused this epidemic has a relationship to this susceptibility. This susceptibility is part of a holistic phenomenon that relates to the patients as individuals and also the patients collectively as members of a society. Those people resistant to the epidemic do not have the same holistic state of susceptibility.

The experience in those parts of the world where homeopathy was common in the 1950's was that the polio epidemic could be treated and prevented with a high degree of success with the homeopathic remedy, avena sativa—made from the oat grass plant. The energy of this plant can cause a reaction in people that is similar to the symptoms of polio. This indicates that as well as the polio virus being common to those people who contract polio, the patients also had an energetic susceptibility that resembled the energy of the oat grass plant.

The homeopathic proving process offers science a tool to further investigate the holistic implications of group susceptibilities as well as individual susceptibilities. The actions of a remedy are defined in a proving by giving it to a group of people three separate times to see what sort of physical, mental and emotional symptoms it is capable of producing. The symptoms produced will then define the clinical usefulness of each remedy.

When a remedy is discovered to be the most curative remedy for a particular epidemic, the holistic implications of that remedy may indicate something about the holistic cause of that epidemic. Remedies are known through centuries of use to be associated with certain influences on people that will cause the appearance of symptoms. This information can be also defined through the proving process.

Comparing the known characteristics of the remedy in people who are susceptible or resistant to the epidemic should result in a statistically significant difference in their physical, mental or emotional characteristics. Those characteristics that are common in the people suffering from the epidemic and not common in those who have no symptoms would give us information about the "group state or consciousness" that predisposed these people to experience the symptoms of the epidemic.

For example, aconite was a common remedy for homeopaths to use in New York City for physical and emotional complaints following the tragedy of 9/11/01. Aconite is well known to treat symptoms of flu associated with a sudden chill. Aconite is also known to create the symptoms of prolonged fear or terror in the people who participated in the initial proving process. There is evidence that your health is influenced both as a unique expression of who you are and also by the influence of the energetic state of groups of people around you who have experienced a similar stress.

If it is true that all healing is self-healing and you create the necessary symptoms to do that, is it possible that we collectively cause diseases to occur and to then be healed? Is it possible there is a collective power to the thoughts and feelings of groups of people that can exert a positive evolutionary influence through the disease process? Is it possible that negative energy can also be additive from one person to another to form a group energy that can be a factor in generating a condition such as an epidemic?

At the least, asking these questions can stimulate thought and this may provide answers with time. For today, the only practical application is to realize you're ok and so is everyone else around you. Finding common ground and working together may accelerate progress for all. This would entail using the challenges provided to you by others for your benefit and seeing the stresses they bring into your life as helpful. *The continuum of healing being proposed to you follows the process of your going from awareness initially to acceptance of the fact you're ok and then to forgiveness.* Determining the influences affecting your health and your subtle energy interactions with those around you can enhance your awareness as the first step in healing.

Your Healing Heart

AWARENESS

All Healing is Self-Healing

Law of Similars =
The Healing Law of Nature

Healing = Transforming
Susceptibility into Resistance

Vital Force = "The Big You"

The Disease of Fear

ACCEPTANCE

Changing Your Perception of Reality

Being Open-Minded to
Alternative Views of Reality

It's OK to Talk to Yourself
and Listen to Your Body

The Amazing Human Being

Western Medicine has Value
as a Healing System

FORGIVENESS

The Meaning of Symptoms and Disease

You're OK

Healing: The Never Ending Story
= Learning and Healing Through
Life's Opportunities and Challenges

Chapter 10

The Diseases of Fear

Learning the principles of energetic and holistic medicine as outlined in the preceding chapters, has prepared you to now look at specific disease states in a new way. This new perspective is based upon both the concepts of healing as self-healing through the application of the Law of Similars and the reality that you have a vast system of energetic controls that is constantly perfecting your state of health. The emphasis in this new approach will be on finding and treating the underlying cause of your symptoms instead of the symptoms themselves. You will then have the ability to devise a treatment plan that permanently removes the symptoms without producing side effects.

Diseases in western medicine are named for their anatomic and symptomatic findings. For example, the disease rheumatoid arthritis describes an inflammatory condition of the joints. In the energetic philosophy of medicine, your diseases become defined differently through understanding the cause of the symptoms. The treatment is then directed at strengthening your resistance to this underlying cause. Diseases will be defined more according to the susceptibility they represent than their anatomical location or symptoms

For the purpose of illustrating this new perspective of the disease process, you will be asked to consider a new category of diseases defined as resulting from experiences that cause a state of fear. Fear is the underlying susceptibility that has been triggered by an event in life. The symptoms that result will vary according to the unique nature of each patient and the nature of the condition that has caused the state of fear. Your reactive, symptomatic response represents the clinical findings and fear represents the cause. The individual patient's treatment will be determined by the symptoms produced as a reaction to the experience of fear.

This new process of determining the cause of the symptoms and the best treatment will be different than what is used in western medicine. Different patients will present with different symptoms even though the cause of the symptoms is the same—fear—because they are unique individuals. The holistic evaluation of this new perspective allows patients to be treated when their symptoms may only be functional and all laboratory testing comes back normal. This process is helpful in patients with chronic diseases and particularly those with autoimmune or malignant diseases when the cause of the disease is not apparent on diagnostic testing.

The process of diagnosing the cause of a disease and determining a treatment that deals with the cause will be different in this approach. The diagnostic rules of western medicine may not apply or be helpful. The thought processes that you were previously comfortable with will now be challenged to see any problem that needs treatment from an entirely different perspective. This takes you back to the original question from chapter one: Is it possible to change your perception of reality and improve your health and enjoyment of life? Yes, it is possible but it is challenging to determine how a change in your perspective will lead to a better understanding of the meaning of your diseases and a more effective treatment to recover health.

From the perspective of a western trained physician, diseases are understood and categorized by lumping all patients with similar symptoms together into broad diagnostic categories such as infectious, traumatic, congenital, tumors, allergic or auto-immune. You are now being challenged to apply the principles of holistic and energetic medicine in a different approach to understanding the cause of each patient's unique symptoms.

For the example of a disease based upon fear to be a meaningful demonstration, a thorough investigation of the evidence supporting it will be undertaken. You will be presented with evidence that demonstrates how a common disease like chronic fatigue syndrome can be a disease whose cause is fear. As an answer to the question of what is the value in changing your perspective; *it becomes apparent that deciphering* **why** a person produces the symptoms of their disease has more importance than the symptoms themselves.

Fear would seem to be more appropriately considered only as a state of mind, but when you evaluate patients holistically you will find common physical diseases associated with fear as their cause. Fear can represent a susceptibility (and therefore a cause of disease) as well as a reactive symptom in response to a stress. You will have varying proportions of physical, mental and emotional reactions to those events in your life that are capable of causing a disease symptoms. The strength of your reaction will vary in all three areas of symptoms but each area will react. Therefore, fear will vary both in the type of influence it has on you and in the type of fear response you make to influences on you.

Your challenge in this study of the diseases of fearwill be to understand the holistic reaction process of how an encounter with an emotional trauma like fear can result in what is thought to be primarily a physical disease. In the common understanding of western medicine, the diseases presented for your consideration would have no known relationship to fear as their cause. The basis for this new perspective on the cause of these diseases can best be established by investigating the nature of those treatments that are found to be the most curative for them. The implication that is inherent when a treatment demonstrates itself to be curative is that it is holistic and it has dealt with the underlying cause of the disease and not just the secondary symptoms.

Before you begin investigating the process of finding a curative treatment for diseases secondary to fear and understanding the mechanism by which fear creates a disease, it might be appropriate to define the word fear. There are several common terms used that can carry the same meaning as the word fear. A mild form of fear could be associated with a state of worry. A more moderate state of fear might be described by the terms anxiety or "being stressed out". Stress is quite a broad term and can also include many other emotional states. The state of mind that you would recognize as one of fear can be experienced in a wide range of severities. A more severe state of fear may be characterized by the terms panic or terror.

Several factors will have implications for the degree of influence a fear producing experience will have on the balance between your state of health or disease. In addition to the intensity of the state of fear you have experienced, the *length of time* that the state of fear has persisted without treatment or resolution will have importance.

You will also have a relative susceptibility or resistance as a natural inclination to the many possible types of fear causing experiences. This inclination will matter greatly in the results you experience following a traumatic event. As your response, fear can dwell in your mind for an extended period of time or the state of fear can be quickly suppressed into the extra-conscious. It is then from the extra-conscious mind that fears influence your health and creates symptoms to help you overcome your fears.

The emotion of fear is likely universal to the human condition. Each individual person has both a unique degree of *sensitivity* to fear and a unique *susceptibility* to specific influences that triggers their fear response. The number of specific situations that can trigger a state of fear is potentially very large. Any one person will likely only be fearful of a small number of that potential.

For example, you could have a strong fear of snakes and also a fear of failure as being the two things that can create a strong state of fear for you. These two things can automatically grab a hold of your energy state. In contrast: a fear of spiders, claustrophobia, a fear of disease or heights will have no power over you at all. It seems that your individual susceptibilities to particular types of fear are just an inherent trait like having blue eyes or brown eyes. Your individual life experiences may enhance a natural fear or introduce a new fear. If you have a near-drowning experience, you may then develop an intense fear of drowning that was not there previously. If you have a natural susceptibility to fear of drowning, a near drowning experience will then have a much greater impact on your health.

If fear is your response to those experiences in life that you perceive as potentially harmful, knowing the specific fears you are susceptible to can help your investigation into finding the individual purpose your symptoms are serving. Fear can then be used to define your susceptibilities. This is an important part of the process of matching you to the energetic treatment that will be most curative. The known history of this matching treatment (remedy) will have holistic implications for your health. Fear can then be used as an example of how an emotional state can coexist with a physical disease and represent the same reaction to stress.

A good place to start your investigation into the state of fear as a determinant of health is to look at what purpose fear could be serving in generating symptoms. Those symptoms caused by fear should be understood as part of the transformational process of healing.

It is difficult to know for sure, but it appears that at the very beginning of life the fetus or newborn does not have fear as an instinctual behavior. Fear is most likely a learned state of mind that comes from having negative or hurtful experiences. Either your conscious or unconscious mind can associate these harmful experiences with the events that immediately preceded the negative experience or the conditions that are present at the time the negative experience occurs.

When a sensation of pain (physical, mental or emotional) is triggered following a particular type of experience, it will reinforce the association between that event and having a fear of negative consequences. Following this event, the energy of fear often becomes directed forward in time in your mind. The consequences of having a fear producing experience will strongly be associated with anticipatory anxiety. Fear is a sequential process of becoming aware that a situation has the potential for harm and experiencing discomfort following the event. The learning is that some type of pain will follow future occurrences of this event.

Fear appears to serve a role as part of your survival instinct. Fear is an adaptive mechanism to help you identify and react to danger. Fear and pain are useful evaluation and defense mechanisms to reduce the likelihood and severity of injury and help to preserve health and life. Pain works at the physical level much like fear does at the mental-emotional level. Both alert us to the potential for harm and can function as a learning tool to ensure survival.

The importance of fear to survival can be clearly seen in cases where a total absence of fear might exist. An absence of fear can cause catastrophe in the child who runs across a street chasing a ball or who steps into a swimming pool that is deeper than their height. You must be taught to fear the consequences of these potentially dangerous actions by someone who knows of the danger. Otherwise you will have to learn this through an uncomfortable experience. It is fortunate you can learn about potential danger in life without having to experience any harm. This is a valuable way of learning to survive but like many other things can be over done.

If fear is helpful and necessary to preserve life and health, then what do the diseases of fear represent? How and when does fear becomes harmful and causes disease will be subject for your study in this chapter. Understanding that fear can be a source of many diseases represents both a change in your perception and the interpretation of the information your body is telling you in the way of symptoms. Knowing the usefulness of fear and its appropriate place in your life may help to transform those situations where it is causing disease back into usefulness. *In examining the diseases of fear, it needs to be clear that fear is not a disease itself, but is a cause of disease.*

Fear represents your response to an event that you perceive as being potentially dangerous. Fear as a state of mind will have a specific duration in time. This event can be dangerous right now or can lead to a dangerous condition in the future. The relationship between fear and an event develops over time. An event may not create fear until negative consequences become associated with it.

The question becomes when does fear produce either an acute or a chronic state of mind and how does the state of chronic fear result in disease? Is there a parallel between the physical states of pain as both an acute and chronic state of the body and with fear as a state of the mind?

When you encounter an event that causes injury, defensively you will try to prevent it from recurring. The amount of fear associated with that event will be proportional to the injury caused by the event and the circumstances that lead to its occurrence. Fear does not occur without some sort of attack on you or the transference from another of fear associated with an event in their life. It would seem that you can learn about fear even without the direct experience of danger. Everyone has a unique degree of sensitivity to fear that determines the strength of the stimulus necessary to induce the fear response. Your balance of susceptibility and resistance to each individual event also determines how you will respond.

If fear is a learned behavior, once fear becomes firmly established through repeat experience, it will become a constant feature of your state of mind. Fear will then either be consciously expressed or will exist in the subconscious mind as a potential state to be expressed either by your body or your conscious mind. Your current state of mind (of fear being either expressed or suppressed) will depend upon when the triggering events associated with fear occur. If the event occurs infrequently, it will be present only at those times as a state of acute fear. The rest of the time it will be subdued in the background as a potential influence on your behavior and health. If the potentially dangerous event is more ever-present the fear will be experiences on a chronic basis. The intensity of your fear response (as symptoms or a disease) will vary according to the intensity of the perceived threat.

To be valid, this model of perceiving the meaning of fear in a way that defines the events in your life as dangerous needs to be consistent with the observed physiologic processes that make up your response to fear. Both the anatomic and the energetic physiology of the fear response should be consistent with this explanation of fear. It can then be useful in defining the diseases associated with fear.

Treatments that are directed towards fear as a cause of disease must be able to affect how you perceive the level of danger in the world. Your treatment will then have the greatest potential for strengthening you and reducing your susceptibility to fear. Curative healing must be balanced. You must maintain a realistic perception of danger to avoid behaviors and situations that are potentially harmful.

Health will be promoted by finding balance between perceiving the world as an overly dangerous place and the opposite overly reckless view of the world characterized by extreme fearlessness. In cases where a disease of fear has already been established, the healing process involves overcoming established patterns of perception. This process needs to be consistent with the principles of healing that have been established in previous chapters.

It will be helpful to look at both the energetic and anatomic physiology of the fear response to understand how fear creates a state of disease. Whether a state of fear protects your health or creates a disease will be affected by several factors. Some of these factors are the strength of the fear-producing stimulus, your susceptibility to that stimulus, your general level of sensitivity and the duration or frequency of repetition of the stressful events. It will be helpful to consider all of these factors in finding your optimal response to potential danger and he best treatment methods that increase your ability to respond to fear in a way that strengthens your resistance to fear in the future.

The gross anatomy and physiology of the fear response is well known as a function of the sympathetic division of the autonomic nervous system. This is the "fight or flight" system that enhances your ability to defend yourself and survive an encounter that is perceived by you as dangerous. The events that can stimulate the sympathetic nervous system to increase its functions include anything that you perceive as dangerous. It can be a physical stress such as being injured in a car accident or a mental-emotional stress such as the sight of your angry boss yelling out your name.

You respond to all potentially harmful events in the same way through the actions of the sympathetic nervous system. Depending upon your individual susceptibilities and the circumstances in your life, many situations that you perceive as adverse can stimulate the sympathetic nervous system to respond (examples could include any physical injury, abuse, abandonment, rejection, loss of support or an environmental stress or deprivation).

When you perceive a dangerous threat to your survival, you may react with fear and trigger a "flight" response. You may also respond to a fear for your survival, or the survival of someone important to you, by initiating an attack or counter-attack response that represents the "fight" response.

When perceiving danger or fear, you will respond by increasing your output of the emergency hormones like adrenalin and epinephrine that activate the body's tissues that enhance your ability to survive the stress. Your adrenal glands respond to the perceived level of threat by increasing the level of these stress hormones in the blood.

These stress hormones will have a strong effect on most of the tissues in the body. The body's response to elevated levels of adrenalin will increase the heart rate and blood pressure as well as shift a greater percentage of the blood flow to the muscles and sensory organs. A lower percentage of the blood flow will go to other organs, like the digestive tract, that are less vital in overcoming an imminent threat.

The common denominator in triggering the sympathetic nervous system is the perception of danger in your environment and it's creation of the mental state of fear for your survival. The physical connection of the sympathetic nervous system between the brain and the adrenal glands represents one mechanism of responding to stress. The actions of the sympathetic nervous system will alter the function of the various tissues of the body in a way that is logical and predictable for survival.

The functions of the sympathetic nervous system are balanced by the parasympathetic nervous system. The parasympathetic nervous system enhances your long-term survival through restorative and regenerative processes of the body's tissues during times of less stress (especially during sleep). The parasympathetic nervous system produces its own set of hormones, noradrenalin and norepinephrine, that have effects on the body's tissues that are opposite to the sympathetic hormones.

In both western medicine and Chinese medicine the adrenal glands are the most vital organ or meridian system responsible for the "fight or flight" response—or your fear response to a perceived danger. In Chinese medicine, the energetic information system responsible for this response is contained in the function of the kidney and bladder meridians.

These paired meridians start in the feet and ascend the leg and penetrate and interconnect the physical organs of the spine, head, kidney, bladder, adrenal glands, brain, lungs, heart, throat and tongue. The functioning of all these organs will be closely related to the body's response to the level of danger that you perceive. The symptoms and signs associated with diseases that have fear as their cause will be expected to have various manifestations in the organs and tissues of the body associated with these meridians.

One function of the kidney and bladder meridians represents your energetic response system when you perceive the events of life as being fearful or dangerous. In Chinese medicine the organs of the body associated with these meridians will demonstrate both the over activity associated with the energetic state fear causes as well as showing the effects of chronic stress depleting the vitality of those same organs.

When the pattern of energetic disturbances seen in the body fits the known anatomic relationships of the kidney-bladder meridian, it can confidently be presumed that the source of your disease is related to fear. This pattern means that you will have an inherent susceptibility to perceiving the events of your life in a way that presents danger or fear and a strong enough event to trigger that fear has occurred.

It is important to understanding *the significance of the association between your body's response to an event demonstrated in the meridians and the known significance and functions of that meridian.* Finding this anatomic pattern helps determine the most powerfully curative treatment for the disease by knowing its cause as fear. It may help to recall the previous discussion of how *only you* give the meaning to the events occurring in your life (rabbit story). If your body demonstrates the kidney meridian susceptibility to fear, you by nature will respond to stress more with fear than other emotions like anger or sadness.

Recurring patterns of diseases or symptoms in your life give clues to understanding where you have the need to transform one of your susceptibilities into resistance. Looking for an association between similar events recurring in your life and new symptoms following them will establish the causal link that defines one of your susceptibilities. Both your past history of when new symptoms developed and the current tissues or meridians producing symptoms provide helpful evidence to find the cause of your diseases.

Your symptoms and signs of disease provide the evidence necessary to achieve the level of awareness needed to begin profiting from the experiences life is making available to you. By attempting to profit from the meaning of your symptoms and not just suffer from them, you can be strengthened and achieve better health and enjoyment if life. The efforts you invest in this process will be returned to you in wisdom and the strength that prevents the need for future symptoms (based on fear or any other cause).

In the search to fully profit from your experience of life, there is also helpful information that can be obtained from studying the holistic approach of homeopathic medicine. In cases where fear is the cause of disease, the homeopathic remedy that best matches your symptoms and results in a deeply curative response can then be studied. Your study should confirm that the underlying susceptibility being treated was that of fear. Certain homeopathic remedies are well known by experience to be related to fear. When a homeopathic proving of them is conducted, they will cause a state of fear to appear in the proving subjects. The use of these remedies in patients affected by fear has a long history of helping these patients recover their health.

You can now see that when taking a holistic approach towards understanding the diseases associated with fear, you can approach the situation with information from several sources. The information should all fit together to provide a greater understanding of the cause and lead to the most permanently curative treatment.

The goal is to combine all these sources of information and achieve more efficiency and power in improving your health: (1) The western understanding of the physiology of the sympathetic nervous system and its effects on the function of the organs of the body. (2) The diagnostic methods of Chinese medicine to indicate which meridian system is the source of your dis-ease. (3) The known holistic implications of the homeopathic remedy that matches your symptoms will indicate the underlying susceptibility.

Together these tools can help you identify a hidden cause of disease that is not easily recognized. The cause of a disease can be difficult to discern for several reasons. The cause can have occurred at a distant time and is not recalled. The cause can be influencing you at the mental-emotional level and be difficult to define accurately or it may have been suppressed out of your conscious awareness.

Making use of all available information will allow you to see patterns of symptoms that recur in a number of patients. These patterns clarify the underlying etiology of several common disease conditions as being based upon a fearful perception of the world. These patients will view the world as predominantly a place of potential danger. It is not very easy to recognize this tendency as a cause of disease until all three of these tools are learned. Once they become familiar to you, they can be used to recognize specific disease patterns by their underlying cause.

Once this multi-faceted approach to understanding the cause of disease becomes a comfortable process, it leads you to *ask several questions about the meaning of fear as a source of disease.* You need to consider *when* does fear become a source of disease instead of a mechanism to protect yourself from danger? If this process happens cumulatively through life, *what* is the influence of your sensitivity to fear and the strength of the stimulus generating the fear? Can fear be experienced and healed as part of a *process* of becoming resistant and strengthened in a way that overcomes your susceptibility to fear in the future? What determines whether fears are *transformed* to strengths in a curative healing process *or* whether they are just *suppressed* out of the conscious awareness and transferred to the extra-conscious awareness to be expressed at a later time in the body as symptoms? *What kinds of diseases* are commonly seen as a result of the experience of fear? What are the common physical symptoms associated with the homeopathic remedies that are associated with the mental state of fear?

The certainty of your answer to these questions will be determined by your level of understanding the principles of western, Chinese and homeopathic medicine that have been outlined. As your expertise increases, so will your accuracy in making a diagnosis and choosing a curative treatment. For your assessment to contain truth it must be able to explain the cause of diseases associated with fear and provide a direct and sure correction. This is the ultimate reason for writing and reading this book. Hopefully, you now have an enhanced understanding of the principles and process of healing.

The concepts of *sensitivity and vitality* are important factors for each individual person in determining when a stress that is perceived as potentially harmful can be a useful protective mechanism to avoid harm and when it might become a source of disease. Since the power of the stresses you encounter in life is not under your control, it makes more sense to try to improve your vitality and sensitivity.

Chinese and homeopathic medicine addresses the topic of trying to build up your vitality through making healthy choices in your life and providing therapies that strengthen the vital force (Chi). Making improvements in vitality will tend to drive your sensitivity towards normal, if it is low or high. You will tend to retain your initial level of sensitivity to some degree. Therefore, it is more important to just become aware of whether you have either an unusually high or low sensitivity. You can anticipate and prevent excessive reactions in your health by being aware of your tendency to over or under react to the stresses in your life.

When you experience a successful adaptation to a potentially harmful event in life (new symptoms are not produced), you will not develop a fearful response to that event in the future. This represents a fundamental shift of power towards you and away from life's events having power over you. This power shift takes you in the direction of health and away from disease. This is the essence of healing as a transformative process.

The process of achieving a response that maintains and promotes better health has inherent in it some measure of time to perceive the event and anticipate the outcome of your response. During this time a decision is made. Your capability to respond in a way that gives you control over the event and minimizes the potential for harm will be learned by experiences with a successful outcome.

A successful encounter with these events provides experience in handling potential danger in a way that is perceived as reinforcing your ability to adapt to events of the world. These experiences give you confidence to continue learning by this process in the future. Your success will be determined by your overcoming the results of past experience as well as your capability (vitality and strength) to be able to control the forces involved in the encounter. This healing process represents transformation from susceptibility to resistance and is most efficiently done with the assistance of the Law of Similars.

When you make an inadequate or unsuccessful response to a potentially harmful event, you are likely to suffer some sort of harm. The physical or mental pain associated with this encounter will also result in learning by experience and fear will be associated with the event. Fear is a mental state that becomes projected into the future as a consequence of a past experience. The painful consequences of your past experiences can cause fear to be associated with any future recurrence of this same event.

There are several factors that influence the balance of whether the events in a person's life will generate more of less fear in their life. Your perception of pain presents a good analogy for your perception of fear. You can almost interchange the two words in the rest of this paragraph. People vary greatly in their sensitivity to fear. People vary in the strength of the stimulus needed for them to recognize it as fearful. They also vary in the magnitude of the harmful effect on the body that the fearful stimulus produces before it is recognized as fearful. People also seem to vary in the extent to which a fearful experience will interfere with their ability to function while the fear is present. Individuals will vary in the amount of fear the body will withstand but eventually everyone develops a decompensation in their function at some level of harm.

An individual's susceptibility or resistance to fear is determined both by their unique nature and by training. Your response to the events in your life will be influenced by the instructions of those around you who have impressed upon you their cautions and fears. It is certainly possible to learn fear of future events from others without ever having any personal experience with them. An event may not have ever caused you any harm but you can perceive of it as being harmful and respond with fear even to the thought of it. Your mentors can have a significant input on your likelihood to having a negative expectation for the experiences you encounter in life.

Based upon this understanding of the ability of fear to cause disease, what are the possibilities then for healing the diseases of fear? How can your perception of events be changed in a way that they no longer are perceived as potentially painful and associated with dread and fear?

It appears that curative treatments are possible for the diseases of fear. Treatments are possible that can remove symptoms associated with fear without any side effects being produced by the treatment. A cure is indicated by the patient's future resistance to recurrences of the same symptoms when experiencing similar stresses in the future. With a curative treatment the patient will also report becoming aware of a healthy change in how they perceive and process their reaction to these same events. Other signs of good health may also result from treatment. Having less symptoms in life and feeling a new power to make a healthier response to the challenges in your life indicates that a curative, transformative process has occurred.

In order to achieve this degree of success, the underlying cause of the disease must be recognized and addressed. The patient's vitality must also be enhanced. This mandates a change in the behavioral response that is learned as the one most beneficial to survival. A successful encounter with stress has to occur and be recognized as such. A new option in dealing with the same circumstances that previously brought about failure or injury needs to be learned as a new reaction pattern to stress.

As an example of the concept of a common disease caused by an excessive reaction to fear, I would like to relate a fairly typical case treated from the perspective of holistic medicine. Joan is a 63-year-old woman who had suffered greatly for much of her life with symptoms of pain and weariness. She had been diagnosed by western physicians as having both chronic fatigue syndrome and fibromyalgia. She was frustrated with the sustained suffering in her life and the inability of a primary pharmaceutical and psychological approach to help her. Her previously prescribed treatments often caused significant side effects and usually did very little to help. She had a lot of counseling and physical therapy treatments without any persistent relief of her symptoms.

After her initial evaluation, it was decided to evaluate Joan's susceptibilities with Chinese medicine. Chinese medicine is very accurate in determining the patient's underlying area of susceptibility that is causing their symptoms. Two important things were identified in the initial diagnostic and therapeutic application of traditional Chinese medicine. It was determined that she is a highly sensitive person to external stimuli and that the kidney and bladder meridians were the original source of her symptoms. Her other organ systems were actually quite well balanced.

The information gained from Chinese medicine was then used to direct the taking of her case in the style of classical homeopathic medicine. A remedy was chosen for her that fit the totality of her symptoms and was well known to have strong actions in the mental-emotional sphere against fear. It turned out that she had been born in London, England in 1940. As a little girl she experienced the terror of nightly bombings. The imminent threat of death and destruction could be seen all around her. Her situation of living in danger was combined with her natural susceptibility to fear and became imprinted on her for the next six decades.

Within the matter of a few short days of starting on the matching homeopathic remedy, her life made a near-miraculous turnaround. She began sleeping restfully without interruptions and was awakening more refreshed than before. Her energy level began to steadily climb to where she could work again without exhaustion and weariness. Her body pains gradually left and she could comfortably return to a normal level of activity. Patients always notice the physical changes most directly, but within a few months she became aware that her entire outlook and perception of her life was changing in the direction of optimism and increased enjoyment of life.

Taking Joan's homeopathic history illustrates well a very common pattern of behavior that develops as an adaptive response to the experience of danger and fear in life. She is a sensitive person, so her response was strong and persistent.

The process of taking the information from several sources together and looking for patterns and logic in the symptoms can demonstrate some realities that were always there to be observed but not recognized. It is especially hard to find these associations if you are looking from the paradigm of a western specialist who will be trained to look for the ever-smallest common denominator in the physical expression of disease. Looking holistically to find the logic behind all of a patient's physical, mental and emotional symptoms can lead to a cure but you need to make use of all the information the body is trying to provide you.

It is instructive to ask patients with a pattern of findings like Joan's, what is the level of control they would like to have over the events in their life. You will find that they almost always have a very high need for control. They can be the true control freaks. There is a natural and logical explanation for this, as well as all symptoms and findings. At some time in their life, their perception of the world as a safe and secure place has been shattered by an event or series of events that introduced them to the concept of harm or danger. Fear strongly influenced their experience of life. Their perception of the world as a dangerous place became the dominant experience. When the world presented to you demonstrates the reality of a potentially dangerous circumstance happening at any time, you will see danger around any corner or in the motives or actions of anyone you encounter.

The urge to survive and avoid pain can overwhelm whatever sense of security you originally came into life with. A complete medical history will often expose the cause and effect relationship behind the patient's symptoms. You will often find an impacting event occurred in the patient's life within a period of months prior to the onset of their symptoms.

It can be incredible exhausting to have to erect walls of safety around yourself at all times. Every time you move or encounter a new situation you will have to recreate or extend these barriers to potential threats. This becomes a strong source of chronic fatigue in those who are chronically fearful. The mental and physical energy consumed in the process of worrying and creating defenses for yourself can be exhausting.

The patient's sensitivity will determine the strength of the perceived threat that they have to encounter. They may not even recall the initial event or they may not have thought it to be significant enough at the time to cause them a chronic disease. The patient's awareness can be greatly enhanced by putting together a time line of the appearance of new symptoms in their life and looking for impacting events in the months prior to the onset of the symptoms.

Chronic fatigue syndrome often represents a disease caused by fear. The patients are consuming large amounts of energy in the mental-emotional state of anxiety and worry. Remember that 30% of the cardiac output goes to the brain. The hyperarousal, defensive state of mind can cause the brain to consume large amounts of energy. Fatigue results as there is not enough extra energy left remaining for other physical functions.

It would be an interesting study for medical practitioners to ask their chronic fatigue patients to rate their level of fear, their need for control in life and their energy level. The recent focus has been on asking all patients to rate their physical pain on a scale of one to ten. It would not take much longer to ask them to rate a few other symptoms and learn some interesting observations.

After stopping the specialty practice of orthopedics and doing general holistic medicine, I was surprised to find a quite similar pattern in other common diseases where the symptoms and meridian susceptibilities were associated with fear. Other common diagnoses from a western perspective that follow the pattern of diseases of fear include fibromyalgia, obsessive compulsive disorder, multiple chemical sensitivity, the strongly allergic patient and other phobic diseases like agoraphobia. OCD and agoraphobia are easy to see the association between fear and behaviors demonstrating a need for unreasonable control. The relationship between fear and allergic patients was less obvious.

Once you have the tools available to correlate patterns of symptoms and meridian abnormalities with events in people's lives, the hidden cause of their diseases can be discovered. For example, it is common to find a very definite pattern of association between patients expressing strong allergic hypersensitivities and a history of exposure to danger or abuse at a relatively young age in their life. Again, in the face of an extremely sensitive patient this abuse might be considered as a minor occurrence in the life of a much less sensitive patient. In the case of neonates with severe allergic symptoms, it has to be considered that they may have even encountered a significant level of stress prior to their birth.

Having an experience with physical or sexual abuse clearly redefines your perception of the world. Situations that should normally be supportive can become especially harmful when the abuser is not a stranger. The abused patient's response to a change in the level of security they perceive in their environment may bring about other reactive states besides fear. The body will demonstrate its other natural susceptibilities and react by producing secondary symptoms and the meridians will demonstrate their involvement in the reaction. The fear reaction may have other co-existing states such as anger, humiliation or any other emotion depending upon the person's nature and the circumstances surrounding their abuse.

The allergic patient also nicely demonstrates the holistic reaction of the whole body to a changed perception of the world. Substances such as specific types of food, chemicals, odors, and pollens that were previously recognized by your immune system as safe parts of your environment will now become recognized as potentially dangerous. The body will initiate an immune response against these substances that they now become recognized as potentially harmful. The immune system redefines that substance as an antigen (harmful substance) and programs an antibody to destroy it. This change in perception results in an allergic reaction that can become a permanent part of your cellular immunity.

Dr. Nambudripad's allergy elimination treatment (NAET) provides tremendous insight into the process whereby the body defines specific items as harmful that have no natural reason to be defined as dangerous. NAET uses kinesiology to find the meridian organ of susceptibility. NAET can also be used to find the defining event that caused the change in allergic sensitivity.

It is not necessary to find the precise event that caused the allergy for NAET treatment to be successful. It is instructive though to know that the body retains a specific memory of the original event that is still causing the allergic reaction. A successful NAET treatment breaks the link between the memory of that event and the secondary allergic response. Breaking this link allows patients to come into contact with substances that have been associated with the harmful event and not mobilize an allergic, immune response. Observing this process take place can be helpful in proving to the skeptics that this process is real and the body has a precise and purposeful reason when it identifies an item as harmful. Your antibody response can be both programmed and unprogrammed according to what your immune system (under the direction of the vital force) determines is appropriate to recognize as a harmful substance. *This observation further confirms the appropriateness of your symptoms and having optimism that your potential to heal is ever present.*

The ultimate point of undertaking such an extensive examination of the diseases of fear is to find a gentle yet effective treatment that will produce curative results. A curative treatment demands that you explore the process of finding the logic and purpose behind your symptoms. Your symptoms demonstrate the natural process made available to you to reach your transformative potential of improved health and resistance.

Most of the diseases associated with fear are chronic diseases. Treatments that do not recognize fear as a large component of the cause of these diseases will not be able to be curative. Treatments that deal only with the secondary symptomatic expression of the disease can work only in a repressive manner. Suppressive treatments contribute to the chronicity of the disease and the necessary appearance of side effects.

In order for a treatment to be curative for the diseases of fear, it must recognize that your perception of certain events in the world has been altered to see them as inherently harmful. One goal of a curative treatment is to transform your perception of the events that previously triggered a fear response. *The transformative process* will empower you to make a healthy response to the same event instead of the event overwhelming you. Past negative experiences must be neutralized and overcome by new health reinforcing experiences.

You need to learn that you have the ability to profit from your experiences of life. This health producing level of *awareness* enables you to accept the circumstances of your life for the potential they have to increase your understanding of life. As a result of this transformation, the balance of control switches back to you. If you need to cross a heavily trafficked road, you need to learn the safe places to cross and the safe times to get where you want to go. Until you learn the rules (healing process) you can be stuck unable to cross for fear of being injured. This inability to succeed in life due to fear can secondarily lead to other negative emotions and symptoms, but fear represents the initial susceptibility.

Working with your symptoms to heal allows the inherent energy of your vital force to be directed towards behaviors that increase your healthy enjoyment of life. Less of the energy and efforts of your vital force will be drained off into symptom producing efforts. A normal result of healing is a significant gain in the energy to enjoy and profit from your life experiences.

Each experience that allows you to learn and demonstrate control over the events of your life for your benefit makes future challenges easier to overcome. This shifting of the balance of power is part of the experience energetic and holistic medicine offers you as healing.

Holistic healing returns your health and strength to reverse the chronic process of the diseases of fear. You will be able to recapture the energy that has previously been drained away in your efforts to survive in the face of danger. This energy gain resulting from increased freedom from fear can wonderfully enhance your joyful experience of life. The feeling of true healing that comes from a curative treatment will be very different than any previous treatments you have received that were designed to work against the body's efforts to heal itself.

The essence of the healing process once again needs to be seen as one of gaining awareness, acceptance and forgiveness. The most efficient and direct path is to combine the knowledge of western and energetic medicine in a way that gets you to the first step of being aware of the cause of your symptoms. Accepting the fact that your reactions to this cause are purposeful and to be worked with and profited from is the next most powerful step towards recovering health. Once you have felt the joy of health and healing it becomes easier to look back on the tribulations of the process with forgiveness. You can now redefine in a constructive way the purpose of all the events and individuals that you previously may have misconstrued as causing you harm or fear. Fear; conquered and forgiven, results in health, joy and peace.

Your Healing Heart

Awareness

All Healing is Self-Healing

Law of Similars =
The Healing Law of Nature

Healing = Transforming
Susceptibility into Resistance

Vital Force = "The Big You"

The Disease of Fear

Acceptance

Changing Your Perception of Reality

Being Open-Minded to
Alternative Views of Reality

It's OK to Talk to Yourself
and Listen to Your Body

The Amazing Human Being

**Western Medicine has Value
as a Healing System**

Forgiveness

The Meaning of Symptoms and Disease

You're OK

Healing: The Never Ending Story
= Learning and Healing Through
Life's Opportunities and Challenges

Chapter 11

Don't Throw Out All of Western Medicine

The system of medicine that is taught in American medical schools is based on observations of the body's physical anatomy and laboratory measurements of its physiologic processes. The patient's state of relative health or disease is determined by a combination of their physical examination and laboratory evaluations, such as blood tests or X-rays. The results of these examinations allow patients to be placed into diagnostic categories of disease and then standardized treatments are prescribed.

In the paradigm of western medicine, *symptoms are understood by both the patient and the doctor to be problems* to be removed with treatment. The symptoms are used to indicate which examinations will be most appropriate to also confirm the patient's diagnosis. The physical exam is often problem oriented and will be limited to the organ system associated with the complaint. Usually there is not the luxury of time to evaluate and consider other organ systems that are not part of the complaint. The importance of making the diagnosis is that the diagnosis determines what will be the recommended standard-of-care treatment for a patient with this diagnosis.

In western medicine the term diagnosis has essentially the same meaning as disease. They both are the designations used to describe the patient's condition based on their symptoms and findings. The diagnosis describes the combination of a patient's presenting symptoms and physical finding.

Once the diagnosis is determined, the treatment automatically follows the accepted standard of care treatment for the diagnosis. There is a generalized presumption of cause for most diagnoses. The cause does not need to be specifically investigated as the treatment is directed more at the symptoms and the diagnosis than at its underlying cause. The cause of the disease is presumed to be essentially the same for most cases of a chronic disease. These causes are divided into categories such as degenerative, infectious, traumatic, auto-immune, inflammatory, or benign and malignant tumors. Standardization of treatment in western medicine minimizes the consideration of individual patient differences within a diagnostic category. Though individualization is lost through standardization, speed and efficiency are gained. Standardization also allows the comparison of different treatments for a specific diagnosis and this aids a western model of medical research.

Western medicine has reached its highest degree of proficiency and success in the treatment of acute medical conditions. Western medicine has tremendous capability, efficiency and power in dealing with acutely developing medical conditions. In an acute medical crisis, the body will be enlisting all its resources to survive and recover. The western system is able to assist in the support of this recovery process quite well. The body's response to an injury or acute disease can be closely measured and controlled to minimize the damage and suffering. The techniques of western medicine are designed to limit the damage to the tissues and in this way can augment the body's process of repair.

The techniques of western medicine are highly effective because in an acute situation the cause of the problem can be clearly defined by history and anatomical and laboratory findings. You will know the cause of your symptoms if you fell and broke your ankle. It can also be quickly determined in the case of a heart attack that there has been an interruption of the blood flow in a specific coronary vessel. Since the cause of the symptoms or disease is clearly known, the treatment can be directed at the initial cause in the process of trying to control symptoms.

In chronic diseases it is *not* often the case that you are aware of and dealing with the primary cause of the disease. You are more often controlling the secondary symptoms produced by the body in response to the cause. In the chronic situation, it may be a much more difficult task than in the acute situation to know the cause of the disease. In the acute situation, the cause is more likely observed and considered in treatment right along will the secondary symptoms resulting from the cause. In the chronic situation, this link between cause and symptoms is usually not readily available.

The close link in time between cause and symptoms in acute disease provides clarity in determining the cause of the symptoms and the cause can be considered in treatment. Western medicine's highly developed ability to measure and control the body's response to the acute situation allows it to evaluate the results of various treatment options. Being able to compare the results of various treatment options and continuing to improve upon them has led western medicine to its powerful reputation in handling acute medical conditions.

The cause of acute symptoms will be particularly evident when the cause occurs on the physical level. If the cause of a patient's symptoms occurs at the mental or emotional level, the circumstances or precipitating factors are more difficult to define precisely. This situation gives western medicine more power and advantage in the physical diseases than the psychological diseases.

A patient's reaction to a situation that causes mental-emotional symptoms to be produced will also vary with factors that are unique to them (recall the rabbit story from chapter 8). The individual symptoms manifested in a patient's reaction to stress do not have to be as individually categorized in western medicine to prescribe therapy. The usual treatments may fall into only a couple of common types (counseling, sedatives or antidepressants). The choice of treatment is not as specifically individualized as is the case in homeopathic medicine. The smaller number of choices for treatment speeds up the process greatly in western medicine.

If you choose the western approach to treatment, where the patient's symptoms are the focus of your concern and treatment, you then have two options for drug therapy. You can choose either pharmaceutical management or the alternative approach of herbal medicine and nutritional supplementation. In comparing the two options of western medicine, the pharmaceutical approach has a few more advantages than disadvantages. Both drug options of western medicine (herbal and pharmaceutical) each have their strong supporters as well as their appropriate indications.

Pharmaceutical medicine has for the most part been better researched concerning the expected actions of the drug, its potential side effects and the parameters of dosing. The manufacturing process is more standardized and predictable. The vast majority of western doctors will be familiar with the use of drugs and have regular access to information sources detailing their actions and side effects.

The use of both herbal products and natural supplements in the western approach to drug therapy has long roots going back into folk medicine. Herbs and supplements clearly can produce a drug-like action in the body that will alter the production of symptoms by the body. In the vast majority of cases, their effects will be primarily a *contrary or anti* action on the body, similar to what occurs with pharmaceutical drugs. Herbal medicine, as commonly practiced in the USA, does not have an action on the body according to the Law of Similars as do potentized homeopathic remedies. Herbal and homeopathic medicines are often lumped together through lack of familiarity with what is homeopathic medicine. They really have very little in common.

Naturopathic physicians receive training in herbal medicine in their training but the traditional western medical schools do not teach physicians about herbal medicine. Only a small number of states allow naturopathic doctors to prescribe treatments, so the majority of Americans will find well trained advice on the use of non-prescription pharmaceuticals hard to find from physicians.

This lack of inclusion of herbal based medicine into mainstream medicine has led to a limitation in the amount of research done with herbal medicines. A lot of the research has been done without good controls and is sponsored by the companies selling the products. The supplement research is not monitored by the FDA as occurs with prescription drugs and the research is not subject to the same peer review process for publication. The information on side effects, drug interactions and dosing are much less well defined. The sources of herbal products and their manufacture are less well standardized than pharmaceutical medicines.

These situations makes it harder to know a precisely correct dose for each patient. The source of the initial product, and how it has been processed, can vary and this may cause differences in the actions of different herbal products. All these limitations in herbal, supplement medicine are not the fault of the natural substances, but only a result of the lack of involvement of mainstream medicine in their development and evaluation.

I have an instinctual reaction that the whole plant or source of the herbal product provides a more natural process of recovering health, but very little hard comparative science is available to back this up. This lack of familiarity on my part may only represent my deficiencies in training and education, but it represents the common state of training among the majority of western physicians. My intuition may also be influenced by effective marketing of the natural approach to healing. Until these deficiencies in research and education are corrected, in many cases the pharmaceutical approach may offer an advantage over the use of herbal supplements when you choose to take a western approach to the treatment of your symptoms.

Another practical consideration that can make western medicine your first choice is availability. Even though it is possible to make a compelling argument for investigating the potential of healing with energetic medicine, it will continue to be the reality for a long time in the USA that it will not be available to patients. There less than 200 fully trained homeopathic physicians in the USA. Physicians fully trained in the art of traditional Chinese medicine are also hard to find. There are many self help books available that would be appropriate to use for acute and minor medical conditions. It would not be appropriate to try self treatment for more severe or chronic diseases. In this case, your best available option will likely be traditional western medicine.

I am a strong proponent of homeopathic medicine, but have to be realistic in an appraisal of the results of treatment. There will always be human limitations in the application of the homeopathic principles. These limitations make it less than 100% effective for all situations. In some cases, homeopathic treatment may be ineffective or at best only supportive and palliative. The results you will achieve with homeopathic medicine will depend upon the knowledge and experience of the practitioner as well as the specific difficulties you have. In cases where a curative response cannot be achieved, the state of suffering demands whatever approach is capable of reducing this suffering. Western medicine may be a better choice to relieve symptoms in this case.

Patients are as valuable as medical school in learning when a specific approach to care will be most appropriate. Early on in my holistic practice, I had a patient, Arthur, come for evaluation and treatment in the terminal stages of malignant melanoma. Arthur came mostly because no one else had anything to offer him and his prior treatments had failed to stop the tumors from spreading widely in the body. His oncologist would not predict the number of days he had left to live but it was likely no more than weeks.

Arthur really needed help. He was in great pain from the expanding tumors and did not have enough energy to enjoy his remaining days. He did not want to have his mind clouded by narcotics and was trying to tough it out. This was the first time I was put in the position of being the primary provider of comfort care to control the suffering of terminal disease. Orthopedists are more often only a consultant for bone pain in this type of case. I tend to be overly optimistic in my assessment of everyone's ability to heal and had to learn to temper my optimism with reality so as not to create further suffering through frustration or disappointment in the face of a failure to cure.

Arthur was a wonderful teacher for all of us at Ohio Holistic Medicine in the art of ending your life in a meaningful way. He benefited greatly from acupuncture and homeopathic remedies in keeping his mind clear and controlling his pain. His strength improved to where he was able to enjoy going back to work for several months without undue strain. He was able to comfortably travel on vacations with his family and have a reprieve from the suffering and the imminent threat of death for a period of about six months. During this time he was able to become comfortable with the end of his life and the future of his family and children in the world without his physical presence.

During the last month of his life, he had to be hospitalized a few times for complications from his disease but responded well enough to return home with his family. A balance between the supportive care from alternative medicine and western medicine was struck where both were utilized when they were the best option. The end of his life came quickly and thankfully. I must admit I felt a little defeated in our attempts to heal him. His wife visited the office a few weeks later and related her grateful appreciation for what we had been able to accomplish in Arthur's behalf. This brought meaningful closure to a learning experience about the meaning of life, healing and health.

The guiding principles you use in choosing a therapy should be to keep an open mind in all directions and to honestly assess the results of any treatment and change where appropriate. Patients should be insistent on getting the best advice possible and motivate their physicians to be as equally open-minded to their potential for healing.

Your Healing Heart

AWARENESS

All Healing is Self-Healing

Law of Similars =
The Healing Law of Nature

Healing = Transforming
Susceptibility into Resistance

Vital Force = "The Big You"

The Disease of Fear

ACCEPTANCE

Changing Your Perception of Reality

Being Open-Minded to
Alternative Views of Reality

It's OK to Talk to Yourself
and Listen to Your Body

The Amazing Human Being

Western Medicine has Value
as a Healing System

FORGIVENESS

The Meaning of Symptoms and Disease

You're OK

**Healing: The Never Ending Story
= Learning and Healing Through
Life's Opportunities and Challenges**

Chapter 12

Healing: The Never-Ending Story

The final chapter of this book should only be the start of your healing journey. The emphasis in healing needs to remain on the time tested principles you can use to free yourself from the burden of symptoms and diseases. Questions relating to the purpose disease serves in your life should now have clearer answers. Not every question has been answered but the healing principles you have learned can be relied on to heal most of the diseases you might encounter.

The emphasis in this book has been primarily on *learning a healing process* that allows you to make the best use of readily available information. This information is available to you through your symptoms. Natural treatments have been emphasized that work along *with* your symptoms to eliminate them. As you review the principles behind the process of healing yourself, it will demonstrate how far your understanding of health has come and how far it can go. As you learn of your amazing powers to create and cure your state of health, try to maintain a balance between an attitude of inappropriate arrogance or excessive humility.

It is important to note the great power you are demonstrating at all times in producing the ideal symptoms and the perfect state of health in response to the countless and varied influences on your health. At the present time, your health is probably somewhere between absolutely perfect and completely hopeless. You may have already overcome quite a number of challenges to your health but you may also be currently suffering the effects of other challenges. Learning and using new tools to move more symptoms from the challenge category into the success category is the motivation for studying the possibilities of energetic medicine.

A goal for your study is to learn the reason why you produce different states of health or disease in response to life's events. The premise is that there is a completely logical reason for each of your responses. To understand the logic behind your current state of health, it helps to search for a repeating pattern that demonstrates a cause and effect relationship between the events in your life and your symptoms. This deductive reasoning can lead you to the truth of why you have the health you do by being consistent with the principles of science (reliability, verifiability and predictability).

You will achieve the best success in this process if you are open to any and all possibilities as being the cause of your symptoms. Being closed-minded limits the pace of your growth in understanding the healing process. Being open-minded also helps to widen your perspective on possible explanations for the cause and effect relationships you observe. This is especially helpful if your current view does not hold out any possibility of explaining the reasons for your symptoms. Getting as close as possible to the truth of the cause for your symptoms increases the likelihood that whatever treatment you chose will be effective.

It takes effort and persistence to understand and implement alternative thought processes when they are different from what is already familiar and comfortable to you. In order for you to leave your zone of comfort, you will need either a strong natural state of curiosity or a serious challenge to your health. When you are presented with a disease for which there does not seem to be an answer or a reason, it may become a particularly strong motivator.

My personal bias is that either your curiosity or an illness can ultimately enhance your understanding of the meaning of health or life. This viewpoint is based upon the experience of observing the interaction of several different philosophies together in an integrated system of health care. It follows a philosophy that you are not intended to enter and leave life in the same state of evolution. Both the experience of comfort or discomfort can stimulate your growth by capitalizing on opportunities or overcoming challenges. Challenges are an integral part of life. Challenges help you achieve growth by profiting from both your successes and your failures.

The most important requirement for making progress in gaining insight into the reasons behind your state of health is to be open-minded. Being open-minded is a little harder than it might appear at first glance. It takes quite a bit of strength of character to be open-minded. Being open-minded involves an honest appraisal of what are your true capabilities and limitations. This assessment should change as you gain knowledge from your experiences in life. It can be hard to acknowledge your limitations or failures. It may even be hard for some people to recognize and profit from their successes.

The process of being open-minded involves being able to assess yourself and various treatment options based upon the relative merits of their ability to produce a successful result. For the purpose of this discussion, it is important to draw a distinction between the process of making an unbiased assessment and making a biased judgment. The terms assessment and judgment need be defined to clarify the process of evaluating the results of treatment. Critically evaluating results and discovering the cause and effect relationship producing those results is the important process to be focused on.

In making an assessment of the merits of something or someone, all pertinent facts should be considered without prejudice. You need to consider the facts contributing to the situation and look openly at the implications of the results. Everything that is affected by it positively or negatively should be assessed. In making an accurate assessment of results and contributing factors, you should know your own biases in order to minimize their effects on the evaluation process. This requires including as many perspectives as possible in viewing the factors contributing to your decision and the results of the actions that were taken.

In contrast to making an unbiased assessment, the process of making a biased judgment of someone or something implies that a decision is made based on only a partial knowledge of the facts involved. A biased judgment implies that decisions are made under the influence of opinion more than from knowledge or a complete understanding of the facts involved. Making decisions in this way implies the presence of doubt or prejudice. Prejudice will be inherent in a situation where you make decisions without an adequate understanding of all the facts involved.

Making decisions based upon bias and inadequate information will create doubt that you have made the right decision at some level of your awareness. This doubt can result in two different behaviors as a response to the uncertainty created in your mind. The healthier response is to be the open-minded and investigate further the specific details involved in making a choice as well as the implications of the result obtained from the choice you made.

An unhealthy response to doubt would be to compensate with a mental state of rigid certainty in the correctness of the decision you made. This rigidity is purposeful to cover up the doubt created in your mind. The intensity of the rigidity correlates with the degree of doubt created and your inability to overcome some form of fear or uncertainty. This fear will limit your ability to be open-minded.

The challenge of overcoming fear and being open-minded to foster your growth and healing can be a difficult one. Being able to admit and overcome limitations in your ability to perceive all the facts involved in a decision is a necessary step in this growth and healing process. The results make it worth the effort.

It will help you make better treatment choices to be open to the possibility that alternative treatment approaches can in some situations be preferable and that there is more than one way of understanding of the cause of a disease. **Try to focus your attention on seeing the difference between the cause of a disease and the reactive symptoms the body is producing in response to that cause. This difference will help you know if your treatment is designed to work with the body or against the body. Knowing the difference will allow you to predict whether the results will lead to a cure or becoming dependent upon the treatment.**

Any treatment you may choose will not throw the vital force very far off track for very long. Taking a thorough patient history can help resolve the challenge of interpreting the actions of the vital force. A real-life example can help illustrate this point. Linda came in as a middle aged woman with a recurrent brain tumor and severe spinal pain. Linda had initially had surgery to remove the brain tumor followed by radiation therapy and chemotherapy. She had also had several unsuccessful operations on the spine to relieve pain in the low back and neck.

When Linda's tumor recurred, she could not safely have any more radiation to the brain. A new treatment protocol for chemotherapy would be very toxic and it was not well known how helpful it might be. The tumor was deeply located in the brain and surgery would not be able to take it all out without seriously impairing her function. In the face of these undesirable options, she wanted to try homeopathic medicine.

Fortunately a good match for all of Linda's symptoms was found and her tumor progressively decreased in size on the MRI scan. Her condition improved for about a year. After a year her tumor began to grow again and her headaches returned. A fresh evaluation of her symptoms indicated a new remedy and she responded quickly to the new remedy with the disappearance of all of her chronic back pain but the tumor did not stop growing.

She needed a second surgery to remove the largest part of the tumor. She was started on chemotherapy after surgery but the symptoms slowly recurred along with the tumor. Healing according to the Law of Similars is going to be very difficult while on chemotherapy, so we now must wait until she finishes her course of chemotherapy and then try to find the symptoms that give us a clue to the cause of her tumor.

There is an as yet undiscovered cause of Linda's tumor that has not been treated. The vital force is determinedly moving in the direction of ending her life and suffering because the underlying cause of the suffering has not yet been uncovered. Her tumor initially responded nicely by almost completely disappearing and then it recurred. Her back pain was dealt with by a different remedy than the one that dealt with the tumor initially. Linda knows she can heal by these experiences, but something needs healing that has not yet been discovered. This frustration produces the stimulus to study and learn more.

Linda's case presents some interesting questions for future study. Even in cases where by experience you know the feeling of healing and the feeling of symptoms, there is a reason for each state being present. Until the evolutionary intention the symptoms represent is discovered, their purpose can only be served by the disease expressing itself. Only this lack of understanding really matters. Even in the face of very great suffering, a block to understanding can remain impenetrable. What a great challenge for the medical profession—to be open minded to our inadequacies in perception of what is right before our eyes.

The increasing number of people living with chronic disease is a testimonial to the fact that anti-treatments are not effective in treating the cause of disease. Many of the treatments for chronic disease are designed only to control the secondary symptoms. More specific and more powerful drugs are continually being developed in medicine to control symptoms. The power and speed with which the body responds to drugs can be enticing. It takes a great deal more time to discover the cause of a disease than it does to just treat its manifestations.

Once begun on a drug for chronic disease, it is not very likely that the use of the drug can be discontinued. The opposite should be true if drugs were really able to improve the health of the population by curing disease. There is an awfully long way to go in reversing the trend towards more powerful drugs and more specific surgeries to maintain a sick patient population. The first step in changing this trend is to be open-minded to the effects of anti-body treatments and recognize the difference between a supportive and a curative treatment.

The ability of medical science to improve the health of the population is a work in progress. This is your stimulus to consider the original question from chapter one: how can a change in perspective result in your health being improved. The answer being proposed to you is: that by *being open-minded to an alternative view of the cause of your symptoms and the solution for your problems -you can open yourself to that "AHA" experience that can propel you towards the answers to your diseases.* Being open-minded opens you up to the possibility of receiving information and then acting on it to bring about the improvements.

What is this "AHA" experience that can be helpful in reaching a breakthrough in your insight? In order to understand how the "AHA" experience can benefit you, you will need to consider the expanded concept of yourself presented earlier as the Big You, or what has been more classically known as your vital force.

The vital force is a part of the human being that cannot be observed or measured. The existence of a vital force is best known through observing its actions in producing symptoms or signs of good health. The vital force is, in its essence, that life force that efficiently directs the processes of life and can be observed to be lost at the time of death. The mechanism by which your vital force continually perfects your state of health by utilizing the vast amounts of data available to it will likely stay a mystery for some time. The best approach for now is to learn the principles of healing indicated by the actions of the vital force and work with its intention and not against your vital force.

The vital force works at the subtle energetic level to control the functions in the body in a way that produces your ideal state of health at all times. The vital force also creates the perfect symptomatic response to events in your life that require a change from the balance that was previously the best accommodation to your life situation. The amount of information it can respond to, and the ways in which the vital force can respond, appear to be almost infinite in its capabilities.

The actions of the vital force appear to be programmed or created in a way that everyone follows the same principles in reacting to events in their life and determining their state of health. If this were not the case, there could be no predictability to the results of either your interactions with the world or to specific therapies. Each person's vital force seems to be following the same set of rules. This rule reinforces the concept recognized in holistic medicine that "we are all one" at some level.

The vital force (Big You) stores an enormous amount of data as your experiences of life and produces a purposeful, healing response to the infinite possibility of events you might encounter. It is beyond our present capability to determine the location of the vital force or its mechanism of action in directing your health. In understanding the vital force, it is possible to use the information gained by observing patterns of the vital force's actions that uphold the criterion of science (measurability, predictability, verifiability, reliability). Learning these patterns allow you to predict the results of your interaction with anyone or anything in the world. The observation that relates to healing is the Law of Similars.

The Law of Similars is probably the most powerful insight that is currently possible for you to achieve into the healing process and knowing the meaning of your symptoms. The Law of Similars may be powerful enough that it is really all you need. Unfortunately, only the results of the application of the Law of Similars are available for study. The force causing the healing reaction is not knowable. The sense you can make of the Law of Similars will not likely be any better defined than its age-old principle (like cures like) established as the fundaments of treatment in the science of energetic medicine. The inability to measure or observe the extremely subtle energetic forces at work in healing will continue to keep the study of healing a never-ending process for some time to come.

At the current time, two divisions of medical science study healing from basically two completely opposite approaches. They are the reductionist approach of western medicine and the holistic approach of energetic medicine. The reductionist approach may succeed in understanding the healing process when it finds a way to measure the very subtle energies used by the vital force. It is likely, in my opinion, that the reductionists will discover the same principles that are used in the holistic approach to understanding healing. If both systems seek and find the truth of healing, they should both "discover" the same principles.

The principles of the hologram may serve as a model for bringing these two opposite approaches to scientific study together into one philosophy. An examination of a holographic picture demonstrates that small parts of the whole picture still contain the information of the whole picture. It is also true that the whole picture contains in it all the information of each small part.

The study of the hologram in physics may help to understand the concept of Eastern philosophy that "we are all one". Each person's field of energy (vital force) may be part of a larger field of energy that allows us to share many things. This may help to explain some of the peculiar subtle energy interactions that people can have at the level of the mind.

If you can accept the existence of a vital force as a part of who you are, you are then recognizing a powerful force as part of your holistic self. This force acts to determine your state of health beyond the awareness of your conscious mind. Both your vital force and your conscious mind play a role in determining the state of health that you experience. You have in essence, two wills that are acting to produce changes in your health that result in the transformative or evolutionary process that is a natural consequence of living. The actions of the extra-conscious will or the power of the vital force seems to always have a positive evolutionary trend towards more joy, comfort and ease as your life experience. The vital force functions to help you profit from the opportunities life brings you.

The conscious mind is more variable in making choices that affect your state of health. Life continually brings you circumstances that require you to make choices. The decisions you consciously make may bring either great joy or great pain. As a right of birth, you have the free will to choose how you will experience life. Therefore, you have to acknowledge that the consequences of your decisions are your responsibility.

Deferring the responsibility for the consequences of your actions to someone else or something else may be an enticing fallacy, but is not likely to fool your extra-conscious awareness. At the level of the vital force (Big You), the true responsibility for your actions is apparent and your state of health will be altered in an appropriate way through the actions of the subtle energy system. Your vital force typically might react by producing new symptoms of a physical disease along with a mental-emotional state of dis-ease (sadness, anger, fear or guilt). Your response will always be holistic.

Accepting the existence of a vital force changes your perception of reality. You will realize that you are much bigger than the awareness of your conscious mind. This awareness will open you up to new possibilities for enhancing your health and enjoyment of life. The more you can profit from the experiences life is providing you, the less likely you are to produce new symptoms or diseases as a response to your experiences or suffer discomfort in the future.

Part of the learning process is to not see yourself as a victim. You are creating your state of health. You are the one that can change your state of health. You have been reading the natural rules this world provides to help you accomplish healing as a transformation of yourself. Shift your emphasis away from looking at your doctor as your healer and just see the medical systems as a tool to help you heal yourself. Carefully scrutinize the results available with the various treatment options you are given. Pursue the ones that appear to be curative because they reduce symptoms and provide you with all the signs of good health that have been discussed.

Understand you can create good health or bad health. You have definite choices: suffering or joy, pain or happiness, guilt or freedom, fear or love, death or life. The endpoint you choose (life or death—health or disease) is not a random occurrence. It is learned and earned.

Consider the difference between treating an acute condition or a chronic one as you learn about the process of healing. With every acute event in your life, you have a choice of reactions. Try to see the acute event as an opportunity to transform yourself to a higher level of health and awareness. You now know processes that can help you work with all the information resources available to you to accomplish this. Each time you live your life in a way you're your reaction strengthens you, it reinforces your awareness that you are designed to heal. Practice, practice, practice. You most productive investments for the long-term are made in your health. Once true healing has been experienced, you will know why.

If you develop chronic symptoms, it demonstrates that your conscious awareness has swung and missed when life brought you the opportunity to hit a home run. Life is generous in giving you many chances to correct your past errors and recover your health. The spontaneous remission cases document this possibility as a reality, even in the face of very serious chronic disease.

It is quite helpful to always ask yourself—why has my health changed? This is a critical step in the healing process—achieving first a state of awareness of the cause of your change in health. Chronic disease represents an opportunity that life has brought you when something has changed in your life and you have not yet recognized it for the transformative potential it contains. Anti-treatments delay healing. Make *awareness* your priority and invest the effort in making a truthful assessment of what has happened in your life, how you feel about it and reacted to it.

It is reasonable to be optimistic. When you combine *awareness* of your reaction to the influences on your life with *acceptance* of yourself and life as ok, it can be a powerfully transformative influence on your health. Any lesson or insight you gain in the process can strengthen you so that you naturally prevent the occurrence of future problems. You may never know the future diseases you have avoided by achieving a state of resistance now, but you can rest assured that your future health will be better.

Learning the behavioral skills of awareness and acceptance do not always come easily at first. You may have to remind yourself repeatedly in the beginning to use your new skills of perception to find the silver lining in the cloud of symptoms you experience. As a general principle, simple is the nature of truth. Looking for the cause and effect relationship between events and symptoms will point you in the direction of the simple truths.

Look for a pattern of cause and effect relationships determining your symptoms in a repeating timeline of new troubles in your life following particular types of events. This pattern will define your susceptibilities and opportunities for growth. Resisting the truth of this association (or persisting in an illusion as your perception of the truth of life) always entails a lot more effort than just admitting the truth and working with it. Deceiving yourself about the truth and how you are responding to life will just get ever more complicated, exhausting and frustrating. Look for and recognize this pattern. Your awareness of it and acceptance of it helps you to put it in the past, to move towards the truth and recover your health.

Each time you achieve success in the process of *awareness* and *acceptance,* you are better able to achieve the third stage in the healing process; *forgiving* yourself and everyone else that is contributing to transforming your health. The act of forgiving is a powerful force in transforming your health. As you are able to become more forgiving it benefits you in two ways. It gives you the freedom to not spend any energy producing negative emotions or behaviors. Forgiveness allows you to see the value, purpose and meaning in all your actions and thoughts as well as all the actions and thoughts of all those who come into your life.

When you release and forgive all those things that you previously perceived as negative influences in your life; your anger, guilt, fear and sadness are discarded along with them. Releasing all this negative energy will greatly enhance your state of health. Being forgiving allows you to experience more of the positive energies that your life events have always had as their potential. The more you can stop beating yourself up and down with negativity, the faster you will recover from your present symptoms and avoid symptoms in the future.

Learning to be forgiving leads to better health through altering your perception of the significance of events in your life. Forgiveness as a growth process is not simply forgetting. Attempting to forget something is just the act of suppressing a state of mind that is unwanted out of your conscious awareness. You may be able to suppress it out of your conscious awareness, but it will be transferred into your extra-conscious awareness.

Forgetting, when it is a suppressive process, will not lead to growth but only the appearance of "unexplained" symptoms. Attempting to forget events that you misinterpret as only negative is a mistake. You will still have the need to learn from your mistakes in perception. A need to forget implies an error in judgment about the significance of events in your life. You have missed whatever profit was to be gained from the experience.

Forgetting is contrary to learning and growth. Evidence has been presented to demonstrate that the events in your life are presenting you with opportunities to gain some improved measure of health, resistance, knowledge or wisdom. Forgetting is more akin to suppression of symptoms and will result in a failure to profit from life. Those events that result in failure will have some level of discomfort associated with them (physical or mental-emotional) now or in the future due to a further need for symptoms.

Instead of attempting to forget unpleasant experiences, it is more helpful to keep them in your awareness. Experiences that are suppressed from your memory are less likely to be profited from. Suppressed experiences more likely need to be repeated until you finally learn the intended message of the experience. It is more constructive to forgive yourself and everyone else involved in an uncomfortable experience. It will be more constructive to recall the consequences of your actions and the actions of others next time a similar situation presents. You are then more likely to have a happy outcome from the next experience. Happiness, resistance and good health result when you have the freedom to choose your response to life from a larger variety of potential reactions to the situations you encounter.

Forgiveness means you do not have to continue paying for mistakes or continue making mistakes. The intention of forgiving is to help you profit from your experiences (transform susceptibilities into resistances). Forgiveness grants others the right to participate in your growth process without transferring blame or negativity for the necessary role they are providing. Forgiving yourself, and others at the same time, lifts the spirits and health of all concerned. As you learn your lessons in life, you participate in a process of learning and teaching that involves many people. Your life and life events are part of a holographic evolutionary process that provides the ultimate meaning behind all your opportunities for growth.

Using forgiveness as a learning, evolutionary tool involves remembering all three steps at all times: awareness, acceptance and forgiveness. *As you gain practice and experience in the process of working with life and with yourself and not fighting against life and yourself, life will begin to appear less accidental.* This knowledge seems to come automatically as a consequence of changing your perception to a more holistic understanding of life. Your holistic perspective allows you to interpret life's events from both a physical and an energetic understanding.

Being aware of the concept of an interplay of your free will and a directing source for evolution requires some harnessing of the individual ego and seeing yourself as part of a much larger whole. Your free will and ego serve their purpose in the process

of evolution but need the balance provided by a holographic perspective of your place in the larger picture that is life. If this is true there are not as many accidents occurring in life as one thinks. It would imply there is a directional flow to life's experiences providing you opportunities for advancement or a setback in life. This new perspective can free you from assigning negative interpretations to these opportunities (blame, guilt and punishment). As life becomes perceived as less threatening, you feel less attacked and have less need to expend energy on attacking others.

These alternative choices in how you perceive the world represent quite profound changes. In order to accomplish it effectively, you will need guidelines and a process. This is the ultimate purpose of studying the principles that can be learned from the paradigm of energetic medicine and the energetic nature we all have as human beings.

Our never-ending study then has the goal of achieving a happy, healthy state. Scientific studies show that happy people are healthy people in both their minds and bodies. Be aware of what makes you happy, it can make you healthy. This is especially true if what makes you happy also makes the others around you happy.

To expect success is reasonable once you learn and practice the rules for success. Miracles can happen. Today's miracles are only a process that we have not yet discovered the rules governing it. In the 21st century the healing process will look very different than the last century. The information age is bringing together knowledge and experience of different cultures. The combination of the knowledge from different cultures can result in a new perspective that does not have the limitations of the more regional perspective of the past century. You, as an individual person, will not have the inertia of the educational bureaucracy of establishment medicine. Collectively you can be the initial driving force to bring about changes on a wider scale.

My personal experience with adapting new perspectives into a medical practice and seeing the results in my patients instill

confidence that we are just seeing the start of what is possible in healing. I have presented a few remarkable examples of patients healing themselves and introduced the concept of diseases resulting from fear as an example of a new way of looking at healing and the cause of disease.

Hopefully, you can personally benefit from the principles contained in this book and take control of improving your own health. The process of opening your mind to new knowledge can improve your health and everyone's health around you. Through the process of healing, we can assist each other in the process of transforming the world to a healthier place.